Das Sreedharan

the new tastes of India

Over 100 vibrant vegetarian recipes from Southern India

Photographs by Pete Cassidy

HEADLINE

contents

For my ever loving mother, who taught me good taste and was patient enough to wake me every fifteen minutes when I was a sleep-loving and lazy child during my school days.

And my father, who guided me to manhood with a smile and opened the doors to food and kitchen for me to help poor Mum who definitely needed it.

And Alison, my dear wife, strength, inspiration and teacher, to whom I owe what I am today.

Also by Das Sreedharan

Fresh Flavours of India

Copyright © 2001 Das Sreedharan

The right of Das Sreedharan to be identified as the Author of the Work has been asserted by him in accordance with the Copyright, Designs and Patents Act 1988.

Photographs © 2001 Pete Cassidy

First published in 2001
by HEADLINE BOOK PUBLISHING

10 9 8 7 6 5 4 3 2 1

British Library Cataloguing in Publication Data for this title is available on request

Art directed and designed by Vanessa Courtier
Design assistant Gina Hochstein
Food styling by Sunil Vijayakar
Styling by Róisín Nield

Colour reproduction by Spectrum Colour, Ipswich
Printed and bound in Italy by Rotolito Lombarda

HEADLINE BOOK PUBLISHING
A division of Hodder Headline
338 Euston Road, London NW1 3BH
www.headline.co.uk   www.hodderheadline.com

foreword

Like almost everybody in this country, I grew up completely addicted to my weekly curry, which was great; but it wasn't until I first met Das and his cooking that I really started to understand the food and culture of Southern India.

The light, fresh style of Southern Indian cooking has completely transformed my opinions of Indian food. Now hooked, I am still learning about the endless marriages of spices and still amazed about the speed, ease and simplicity of cooking these regional dishes which are perfect for home cooking. Das relies on clever shopping rather than laborious preparation.

The New Tastes of India is a really wicked book with amazing stories and recipes. Dip into it frequently and allow yourself to be transported to Das's homeland: the lush, green, tropical land of Southern India, with its paddy fields and coconut groves, and canals running to the sea. I hope this fantastic cookbook helps you – as it has done for me – and you'll see how easy it is.

introduction

My birth, childhood and adolescence were all spent within the postcard beauty of Kerala, India's lushest southern state and one that is as fascinating to locals as it is to outsiders. Kerala is a land of peace and plenty, where nature plays a prominent role in daily life. The stillness of the lagoons and backwaters, the fresh earthy scent of new grass at the break of the monsoons, the bronze glare of the temple lamps at dusk, the sound of the conch shells echoing in the sanctum – these memories are etched in my mind and forever a part of me even though I am now based in Britain.

The essence of Kerala is its diversity. There are myriad dialects, religions, traditions of dress and, yes, styles of cooking. Distinct differences can be found even within a half-hour bus ride at only 30 kilometres per hour! Yet much of the beauty of the land comes from the centuries-old co-existence of its people and their acceptance of one another as roots of the same tree.

My experiences travelling across Kerala have educated me enormously. I have learnt respect, tolerance, humility and, above all, warm hospitality, a virtue dying across our planet. Even at the small, unnamed teashop under the village banyan tree, you will find a warm welcome and an eager group of locals ready to share the latest news and a steaming cup of tea. Although I have now also travelled across the world to learn the science and art of my trade, it is Kerala that has taught me genuine warmth of service. The satisfaction that I see on people's faces really is worth more than market share.

In Kerala, every occasion – even one of the tiniest significance – demands a feast. It is non-negotiable! This is especially so for the elders in the community. Regardless of their religious preferences, they are all still of the stern belief that it is God's will that guests be fed a meal before they leave the house. It is an act of fulfilment, an expression of prosperity and a display of the family benevolence. Not one auspicious ceremony passes without the faithful being fed – it's a tradition that continues to this day, although the size of the cooking vessels has reduced considerably since the loss of patronage from the rajahs.

Although feasting is such an important part of Keralan culture, not all our cooks can claim to be famous for them. There is an art to capturing flavour and arousing divine aroma in a variety of dishes – sometimes as many as twenty-five to a meal. It is a gifted talent that comes to few. My grandfather was one such cook and I vividly recall the times I tried to wake as early as 4am just so I could sit speechlessly in the corner of the smoke-filled kitchen watching him cook. I guess that is where the seed of my restaurant career was sown.

My mother nurtured this seed and watered it until it grew into me, my thoughts about food and my restaurant business, Rasa. For me today, just as in Kerala, each meal needs to be a feast – an experience to savour and remember until the next one comes along and surpasses its brilliance. Yet the art of cooking is simple and needs to be so. My vision of Rasa is built on this simplicity, as are the recipes in this book. I hope you enjoy them.

Ingredients

It may seem as though Keralan and other Indian dishes require an extensive array of spices and other ingredients. Look closely at the recipes, however, and you will see that most of them contain the same basic flavourings used in different proportions. Brown mustard seeds, dried red chillies and curry leaves are particularly important, so if you want to begin your exploration of Keralan cuisine with just a few spices and herbs, buy those first.

Asafoetida is also known as hing and is an essential part of Indian medicine as well as cooking. It is a milky gum that comes from the roots of a plant native to Northern Kashmir. When fresh it is white, but gradually turns pink then reddish brown on drying. The most common form of asafoetida is a dried yellow powder specially prepared for use as a cooking ingredient. It is used as a final tempering ingredient in many Indian savoury dishes to complete the flavour or enhance a strong taste, but we in South India fry it earlier in the cooking process to overcome the powerful smell. It is thought that eating asafoetida and butter as the first food of the day helps to make musicians' voices melodious.

Bhindi is the Indian word for okra or ladies' fingers. It is available fresh and frozen in many supermarkets these days, where it is most commonly called okra. When chopped and cooked for long periods (as in American gumbo), it takes on a slimy texture that helps to thicken the dish. In South India, however, okra is typically cooked quickly by stir-frying, which gives it a delicious crunchy texture that many people who previously thought they did not like okra really enjoy.

Black sesame seeds are more strongly flavoured than white sesame seeds. South Indian people prefer the former, North Indians the latter. Black sesame seeds have a dramatic nutty sweet taste that suits many sweets and snacks. Try them in pappadavadai – a good example of how few seeds are needed to give a really full nutty flavour – and you'll see why we like them. Black sesame seeds are available in most Asian stores, but if you can't find them, these recipes will work with white seeds, which are widely available in supermarkets.

Cardamom is native to India and used in sweet and savoury dishes as well as drinks. The spice is fragrant rather than hot and usually takes the form of black seeds inside pale green pods. The pods are cracked and used whole in some dishes, rice ones in particular. Otherwise the seeds are removed and ground to a powder that can be sprinkled raw over food as a flavouring and garnish. Don't buy ready-ground cardamom as it loses its flavour and fragrance too quickly to make it value for money.

Cassava is a root vegetable also known as tapioca, but don't confuse it with the fine balls of tapioca starch sold for use in milky puddings.

Chana dal is also known as gram or Bengal gram. These plump, matte yellow lentils resemble ordinary yellow lentils but are bigger and brighter and have a nutty sweet aroma. Chana dal is often described as the festival dal of India. In Kerala, it is associated with the harvest festival of Onam, and especially with the preparation of Kadala parippu payasam (chana dal pudding). Chana dal can be stored for three or four months in an airtight container and is available in most supermarkets.

Chat masala is a salty-yet-sweet spice mix usually made from black and white salts, chilli, ginger, dried mango and a few other flavourings. It is often used as a seasoning for snacks, as well as in salads and with yogurt. Look for it in specialist shops.

Chillies Many people find the wide variety of chillies available quite confusing. Which one should you use for each dish? What if the dish is too hot? In Keralan cuisine, the use of chillies is very easy to understand: we only use two types, fresh green chillies a few inches long, and the short dried red chillies that are only an inch or so in length and sold alongside dry spices. A key technique we use to give dishes the flavour of fresh green chilli without intense heat is to slit the pod lengthways and place it in the pan whole, rather than slicing or chopping it.

Coconut is revered by Indian people as the fruit of the gods and is grown in abundance in Kerala. The crunchy white flesh is deliciously sweet and nutty and is used in savoury dishes as well as desserts and snacks.

Curry leaves come from the kariveppu tree and are used as a herb in cooking. Frying the leaves brings out their nutty flavour and makes them pleasantly crisp. An additional benefit is that eating curry leaves is said to enhance hair growth. They are readily available in Asian grocers but are increasingly to be found in regular supermarkets too.

Drumstick is a very long, thin green vegetable with an inedible, woody exterior. Getting to the fleshy interior invariably involves eating with your fingers and discarding the fibrous outer layers.

Fenugreek is called methi in India. It is an ancient spice, used both as food and medicine. In South India we generally use fenugreek seeds in cooking but in the North they eat the leaves as a green vegetable. The small, hard seeds are one of the most powerful spices and have a strong bitter taste and an aromatic odour, rather like the smell of a curry. In Kerala we often use fenugreek for pickles and for seasoning dishes on completion. Even if a recipe calls for ground fenugreek it is better to buy the whole seeds then toast and grind them to a powder. It is too easy to spoil dishes with the bitter taste of ready-ground fenugreek.

Ghee is the Indian version of clarified butter and now widely available ready-made and sold in tins in supermarkets – look in the gourmet section if you can't find it amongst the Asian spices and sauces. Ghee is a staple ingredient of North Indian cooking but is not often used in South India, except in puddings and sweets.

Gram flour is made from chickpeas and also known as besan. With its dull yellow colour and heavy nutty taste, it can be used in many ways in cooking. In South India we use it primarily in batters for crisp pakoda snacks. North Indians use it as a thickening agent for curries; it is also a main component of the sweet laddu. Gram flour is available in most supermarkets and Asian grocers and can be stored in airtight jars for around six months.

Jackfruit is a very large fruit with a thorny skin, fleshy interior and large seeds. When unripe, it is green but as the fruit ripens it turns soft and golden and its strong sweet fragrance fills the air. Jackfruit is used as a vegetable for curries when unripe, and when ripe is turned into jam by cooking it with ghee. The ripe flesh is extremely sweet and also eaten raw. Once the fruit is ripe it is important to use it quickly because the smell is not something you can get rid of easily. You can get rid of the white sticky paste that oozes from the skin by using a little oil and soap. It is hard to find fresh jackfruit on a regular basis but I have seen it in markets and specialist Asian shops. Many Asian and Thai supermarkets sell canned jackfruit, which is acceptable for making desserts.

Jaggery is a dark, sticky and crumbly sugar made from the juice of crushed sugar cane. Brown or demerara sugars are not really appropriate substitutes because they don't have the same musky flavour, but the recipes in this book will technically work if you use them.

Mango of all varieties are used ripe and unripe (green) in Keralan cooking. When using green mangoes for recipes such as curries and pickles, it is not necessary to peel them as the skin will add a good flavour to the dish.

Masoor dal or red lentils are the most common lentils in North India and the easiest to use for a quick dal curry. When whole, they are dark green in colour, with a round

and flattish exterior. The mature seeds are dried and threshed, then the shell-clad lentils are split to reveal the red lentils. Red lentils are widely available.

Mung beans are called moong dal in India. They are one of the most versatile pulses and come whole or split. Whole mung beans have a good strong flavour but require overnight soaking before cooking; the split ones are easier to cook and do not need soaking. Mung beans are also available 'washed' to remove the green shell. The beansprouts widely available in supermarkets for stir-fries and salads are actually sprouted mung beans, but in Kerala we normally cook whole mung beans as a thoran. The washed variety is used for the dessert paripu payasam (mung bean sweet). Whole mung beans are easy to find in regular supermarkets, but you will need to go to an Asian grocer for the other varieties.

Mustard seeds are fundamental to Keralan cooking. We use the brown variety that can be found in most supermarkets. They pop when heated, a sign of when to add the next ingredients.

Paneer is a fresh Indian cheese with a rather firm texture that allows it to be cut into cubes and fried or grilled. Although 'cottage' and 'curd' cheese are terms often given in other books as translations, these soft cheeses are not acceptable substitutes. However, paneer is now made by a large dairy company in Britain and is widely available.

Papaya, like mango, is used in savoury dishes as well as sweet ones in South India. For vegetable curries you need to purchase green unripened papayas. Desserts and drinks require the ripe golden fruit.

Plantain is similar to banana but has a thicker skin and a starchier, less sweet flesh. It is used widely in South India, where many varieties are grown. For curries, use green, unripened plantain.

shallots (see page 76)

Rice flour is commonly used in breakfast dishes in South India, particularly in batters and doughs, and to make the soft rice noodle cakes idiappam. It can also be used as a thickening agent very much like cornflour or gram flour. You can make rice flour yourself but it is a laborious process: you have to wash basmati rice thoroughly a few times, soak it, then make sure it is thoroughly dried and grind it to a fine powder. It is easier to source the ready-made flour in supermarkets and Asian shops.

Snake gourd is known as padavalanga in the Malayalam language and is perhaps the most unusual vegetable in all of South India. It is long and green and looks like a snake. Inside there are seeds that are slightly larger than pumpkin seeds, and these are removed when we start to cut the vegetable. Snake gourd is extremely easy to cook and becomes very soft when done.

Tamarind is a tangy tropical fruit used as a sweet-sour flavouring agent with a role not unlike that of vinegar or lemon juice. The instructions in this book suggest using compressed blocks of tamarind pulp and dissolving the flesh in hot water to give a tamarind-flavoured liquid to cook with. Ready-made liquid concentrates are available in shops but they tend to have an unpleasant 'factory' flavour.

Toor dal is a type of yellow lentil more popular in North India than the South. It has a pleasant nutty flavour. In the South we prefer an oily, glossy variety of yellow lentil that has a longer shelf-life. Keralans use yellow lentils only occasionally, in dishes including sambar and rasam. In the UK, both varieties of yellow lentils can be bought from Asian stores. Soak oily ones thoroughly in hot water for 10 minutes and wash three or four times to remove the oil before use.

Urad dal are skinned and split black lentils. They add a nutty flavour and crunchy texture to dishes such as medhu vadai and are also ground to make dosa batter. Unlike South Indians, the Northerners tend to use whole black lentils in cooking.

Kitchen equipment

Most Western kitchens need no special equipment in order to produce good Indian food, but there are some traditional items keen cooks may wish to buy in order to achieve authentic results, particularly with some of the lesser-known dishes.

Grinders and blenders Many dishes in this book require that spices, and other ingredients such as rice and coconut, be ground into a fine powder. Sometimes the ingredients are mixed with water, then ground to a smooth paste. Traditional Indian cooks have many forms of grinding equipment, but I'd say the stone mortar and pestle is most commonly used. They come in different shapes, sizes and materials and can be used to pulverise small dry spices and seeds as well as larger ingredients such as dried chillies. A grinding stone is another popular item used for grinding rice and lentils to a fine paste. I strongly recommend non-Indian cooks have a mortar and pestle in their kitchen, even though most of the grinding and blending for our cooking today can be done easily and quickly with an electric blender, food processor or coffee grinder. A clean electric coffee mill is best for dry spices; a blender is best for wet spice mixtures.

Coconut grater A coconut grater is essential to the traditional Keralan kitchen because we use fresh coconut in so many of our dishes. We call the grater a chiraka but it is a large piece of equipment quite unlike a cheese grater. You sit at a wooden seat that has a knife-like attachment covered in spikes. As you turn the handle, it scrapes out the white kernel of the coconut. Modern coconut graters, which are widely available in Indian shops, may not be as sharp as the old ones but they do the job. Alternatively, you can use dried or desiccated coconut in the recipes in this book.

Frying pans Tempering and toasting spices and other ingredients in a small, heavy-based frying pan is much more convenient than using a wok or saucepan. The frying pans can be heated without any liquid or fat and tend to hold the right temperature. They should never be scrubbed with abrasive cleaners.

Kadai The kadai or cheena chatti is an Indian version of the Chinese wok. Traditionally made of iron but also available these days in aluminium and stainless steel, it is deep and curved at the bottom, with a pair of handles on diametrically opposite points of the rim. Kadais are used for both deep-frying and stir-frying and are available in many general kitchenware shops. A wok is a good substitute.

Tawa Made of cast-iron, this slightly concave griddle looks a little like a skillet. It is used for cooking dosa and flat breads such as chapatti and paratha. The tawa can be a very temperamental piece of equipment if it is not treated the right way and demands a precise cooking temperature. In particular, if it is too hot your dosa will be ruined. Never put the tawa away without seasoning it with oil – this helps to prevent rust. A griddle or cast-iron skillet can be used instead of a tawa.

Three-mould appam griddle This piece of equipment is only used to make sweet neyyappam. Traditionally called an appam chatti, it is like a small kadai, not very deep, and has three or more mould holes to create a nicely rounded shape for the sweet. A hot neyyappam chati with enough ghee effectively deep-fries the batter, which then comes out in the shape of the mould. Unfortunately, they are not readily available in Britain but you can use a frying pan or wok to cook the sweet – simply shape the neyyappam batter into balls before dropping it in the cooking fat.

Idli moulds and stands Idli moulds are available from Indian grocery shops. They are specially designed, individual concave moulds in which idli batter is cooked. Made from stainless steel or aluminium, the idli stand or tree has

kadai or cheena chatti, an Indian wok

three or four tiers and allows you to cook several idlis at once. A single-layered idli stand resembles an egg poacher with a central stem and allows you to steam the idlis in a large saucepan of water.

Murukku and sev moulds Both these snacks are made with the same press, a sevanazhy, as we call it in Kerala. Traditionally made of wood, it is a two-piece, hand-held press used to squeeze out batter into vermicelli-like threads. Thin metal discs with perforations of various designs are inserted at the base of the press to produce attractively shaped threads. A large hole is normally used for murukku while the hole for sev is very small. In most cases, an icing bag with different shaped nozzles is a useful substitute. These days you can find metal presses in most Indian shops – buy different designs to make snacks of various shapes.

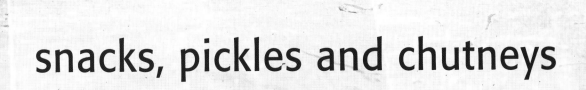

snacks, pickles and chutneys

bar snacks

In our traditional bars, called kallu shaap, people used to while away the hours drinking toddy, but things have changed in the past 20 years. Now even small Keralan towns have plenty of modern bars. These are small, smoky and crowded and sell a variety of drinks as well as interesting bar snacks. The food is highly authentic and very nicely spiced, a perfect match for alcohol.

It is still a surprise when you see local people walk into a bar just to eat the food even if they don't drink alcohol. I was one of those until I started to drink the occasional beer. In those days it wasn't easy to hang around bars because it wasn't considered morally correct.

For vegetarians, bars are not the ideal place for a meal because the menus tend to have a lot of meat and chicken. However, I love the peanut masala, savoury mixtures and pappadavadai served with pickles. They may be light snacks but are excellent any time when freshly made and, although very popular, are not normally cooked in the home. No wonder, then, that I've found more and more family-style bars opening on recent visits to Kerala.

The food in these places is real, and very different from that served in restaurants and hotels. The cooks are from local kitchens rather than catering colleges and maybe for that reason their interest is in flavour rather than presentation. They seem to have more passion for food and knowledge of traditional cooking, and the results are amazing, especially when enjoyed with a big bottle of coconut toddy.

Pappadavadai

Poppadoms are one of the most popular snacks in India and eaten throughout main meals. These ones from South India, which are better tasting and more filling than those you may be used to, have a crunchy masala coating and make a fantastic teatime snack, especially with coconut and tamarind chutney *(see page 38)*. My dad is a master at making them; they were sold in our family teashop from glass bottles at the front of the store and were the most asked-for item we sold. The crunchy sesame flavour and the crackling noises made when people eat them are unforgettable.

serves 4

200g/7 oz rice flour
1 tablespoon black sesame seeds
1 teaspoon cumin seeds
vegetable oil, for deep-frying
100g/3½ oz plain poppadoms

In a large bowl, combine the rice flour, black sesame seeds and cumin seeds. Slowly add 570ml/1 pint of water, stirring to make a thin batter.

Heat the oil in a deep-fryer, wok or large heavy saucepan. Place the poppadoms in the batter and dip to coat them completely.

Fry the coated poppadoms one at a time for 2 to 3 minutes or until golden. Remove from the oil and drain on kitchen paper before serving.

Peanut masala

For most vegetarians in Kerala, peanuts form an important part of the diet and plain boiled peanuts sprinkled with salt and chilli are commonly sold from small wooden carts by eager vendors. When visiting toddy bars or pubs, you are always greeted with a peanut masala such as this one. Despite the use of fresh ingredients, the resulting peanuts are dry and have a spicy flavour that goes well with alcohol. Peanut masala, which is very quick to make, is my favourite snack and often the only vegetarian option offered in Keralan bars. It goes well with beer and, because it is not deep-fried, it's nutritious too.

serves 4

100g/4 oz peanuts
50g/2 oz shallots
1 small tomato
1 fresh green chilli
2 tablespoons vinegar
½ teaspoon chilli powder
2 tablespoons finely chopped coriander leaves
juice of ½ lemon
salt

In a dry frying pan, toast the peanuts for 5 minutes over a medium heat. Set aside to cool, then skin the nuts.

Dice the shallots and finely chop the tomato and green chilli. Place them in a large bowl with the peanuts, vinegar, chilli powder, coriander and salt. Add the fresh lemon juice and mix well.

Keralan savoury mixture

This crunchy, spicy snack is widely known as 'mixture' in India and each region has its own version. It is a speciality of Keralan bakeries, in which you can also buy freshly made vegetable puffs and samosas. The aroma that comes from these shops is unforgettable. The first time I tasted this one was when my cousin Prasad, now chef at Rasa N16, made it for a festival. Since then I have eaten versions of it all over India and abroad, but I think nobody makes it as well as him. Whenever I fancy a mixture, I run to Rasa N16 and he makes it for me. If you can't get it right, you should go to him too. Any type of nuts or crisps can be used in this recipe.

serves 4

100g/3½ oz chana dal
275g/10 oz gram flour
100g/3½ oz flaked rice
100g/3½ oz peanuts
10 curry leaves
2 teaspoons chilli powder
a pinch of asafoetida
vegetable oil, for deep-frying
salt

In a dry frying pan, toast the chana dal until golden, stirring frequently, then set aside to cool.

Place the gram flour in a mixing bowl with some salt and gradually add just enough water to make a soft dough, mixing well.

Heat some oil in a kadai, wok or large, heavy saucepan. Working in batches, press portions of the dough through a sev mould and fry until golden. Drain the sev on kitchen paper and set aside.

Using the same oil, fry the flaked rice and peanuts separately until golden. Drain each thoroughly.

In a large mixing bowl, combine the toasted chana dal, sev, flaked rice and peanuts.

Heat 1 teaspoon of clean oil in a small saucepan and add the curry leaves, chilli powder and asafoetida. Sauté for 2 minutes, then pour the contents of the pan over the sev mixture. Toss well and season to taste.

Leave the mixture to cool, then store in an airtight container.

Kappa vevichathu

Made from tapioca (cassava), this simple snack dish can be prepared by anyone. In Kerala, it can be found in most shops and is very popular in the kallu shaap as it goes particularly well with their lager beer and coconut liquor. It's similar in style to the spicy dry meat dishes served in these bars and is a good vegetarian alternative. Tapioca is ordinary people's food in Kerala and is often preferred to potato, to which it has a similar texture. This dish can also be served as a dry vegetable side dish.

serves 4

500g/1 lb 2 oz tapioca, diced
2 tablespoons turmeric powder
2 tablespoons vegetable oil
1 tablespoon mustard seeds
5 curry leaves
1 tablespoon urad dal
1 tablespoon chilli powder
1 dried red chilli
1 small onion, finely chopped
3 tablespoons freshly grated or desiccated coconut
salt

Place the diced tapioca in a large saucepan and cover with water. Add the turmeric powder and some salt and bring to the boil. Cover and cook for approximately 30 minutes or until the tapioca is cooked. Drain and set aside.

Heat the oil in the pan. Add the mustard seeds and, as they begin to pop, add the curry leaves, urad dal, chilli powder, dried red chilli and a little salt. Cook, stirring, until the urad dal turns golden.

Add the onion and continue cooking for 5 minutes or until the onion is soft. Add the cooked and drained tapioca, mix well, then stir the coconut through the vegetables. Serve hot.

Murukku

This is a small dry snack, almost like savoury cheese sticks, that is served in Kerala with tea in the afternoons. Unlike most of our teatime snacks, it can be kept for some weeks once made. We normally make it in stick form but the mixture can also be shaped into coils. Large murukku coils are a popular food gift and displayed next to the stage at Brahmin weddings as a gift from the bride's family. Restaurants often serve mini-coils but I prefer sticks as they are easier to serve and eat. Murukku moulds can be bought in Indian grocery shops.

serves 4

225g/8 oz rice flour
25g/1 oz urad dal powder
120ml/4 fl oz coconut milk
1 tablespoon sesame seeds
a pinch of cumin seeds
vegetable oil, for deep-frying
salt

Toast the rice flour and urad dal separately. Sift both through a fine sieve into a large bowl. Meanwhile, in a small saucepan, bring the coconut milk to the boil.

Add the sesame seeds, cumin seeds and a pinch of salt to the toasted flour and mix thoroughly. Carefully add the hot coconut milk to the mixture and stir to make a smooth dough.

Knead well until the dough is soft enough to press through the murukku mould. Heat the oil in a deep-fryer, wok or large, heavy saucepan. Press the dough through the murukku mould into the hot oil and fry until golden.

tiffin

My experience of tiffin began at a very early age at my father's teashop. True 'eating out' in India is not geared toward restaurant meals but a variety of snacks eaten throughout the day. We used to open our shop at five o'clock in the morning with light breakfast dishes and go on until late in the evening, changing the menu of snacks according to the time of day. We had an amazing number of repeat visits: the same people would come at various times during the same day to eat the different snacks we were offering. Even though cooking is a regular and never-ending duty at home, it seems Indian people still can't resist the temptation of snack places. They visit not just with the intention of eating, but to take part in the teashop culture and its talking sessions.

Being stuck in the kitchen peeling onions, cutting chillies and grinding rice and lentil batters for making crispy hot snacks like vadai and dosa, our fun was listening to people in serious, loud conversation about the news of the day and problems in America and Russia. Even with the noise of grinders and busy cooking, our ears were always following the discussion and movement in the dining area.

I also associate tiffin with the train journey from Cochin to New Delhi. Railway canteens are famous all over the country for their South Indian food. The Cochin–Delhi trip is too long and homemade snacks are in plentiful supply on the train. People keep exchanging food and in doing so build new friendships. This was very useful on my first trip outside my hometown. It wasn't easy, not knowing any other languages or having any experience of the world – that is, until I met a stranger offering some food. He introduced himself, we became good friends and were in contact for years. Since then I have met many people in this way during my travels up and down the country.

Making tiffin is a daily activity in India. People carry the snacks to work, or take them home after work to please the family; the snacks bought from a teashop are considered special and different from what mothers make at home. To me, teashops and snack food are very much part of our past. Through my restaurants, I have made a humble effort to recreate that diminishing part of our village's culture.

Plain dosa

Dosas have been one of my favourite breakfast dishes since the age of five. I used to go to Dad's teashop at five in the morning and queue up for garam-garam (hot) dosa with freshly made coconut chutney. When Mum makes dosas at home, she sprinkles ghee on them to give a lovely golden texture known as 'ghee roast'. This recipe can also be enjoyed as bread with curries or side dishes. Most Indian people will choose to have potato dishes with dosas. To prepare the batter is time consuming, but cooking the dosas is easy once the griddle is at the right heat.

serves 4

295g/10½ oz long-grain rice
75g/3 oz urad dal
½ teaspoon fenugreek seeds
vegetable oil, for frying
salt

In a large bowl, soak the rice for at least 8 hours in a generous quantity of water. At the same time, in a separate bowl, soak the urad dal and fenugreek.

Drain the rice and dal, keeping them separate. Place the rice in a blender and grind for 2 to 3 minutes, slowly adding 125ml/4 fl oz of water to give a smooth paste. Transfer the paste to a large bowl.

Rinse out the blender, and then grind the urad dal and fenugreek for 5 minutes, slowly adding 4 tablespoons of water, to make a paste. Add the dal paste to the rice paste and mix well. Stir in some salt, then cover the bowl with a damp cloth. Leave to ferment for 12 hours, during which time the batter will increase in volume and become a mass of small bubbles.

When ready to cook, add a little water to the batter to give a thick pouring consistency.

Heat an iron griddle or large, heavy frying pan until very hot. Lightly grease the pan with oil, then pour on a ladle of batter and use the bottom of the ladle to quickly spread the batter out thinly using a spiral motion. Brush the edges of the dosa with a little oil and cook for 2 to 3 minutes until the bottom of the dosa is crisp and golden.

If you are using a filling, add it to the uncooked side of the dosa, then fold and serve. Otherwise, turn the dosa carefully using an egg slice or spatula and cook for another 2 to 3 minutes on the other side until golden. Serve immediately or the dosa will become limp and soggy. Repeat with the remaining batter.

Kochi dosa

World-wide, this is perhaps the most famous South Indian dish, a paper-thin pancake made of rice and black gram, folded in half and filled with a mixture of potatoes, onion and ginger. It can be eaten at any time of day but in certain parts of Kochin is made especially for festivals and celebrations. This particular recipe is a contribution from Rasa restaurants to the dosa family. We add our favourite black eye beans and green peas to the filling, making it an ideal dish for vegetarians and people who enjoy pulses.

serves 4

1 quantity plain dosa (see opposite)

for the filling:

2 potatoes

50g/2 oz black eye beans

50g/2 oz mung beans

6 tablespoons oil

1 teaspoon mustard seeds

10 curry leaves

2.5cm/1 in fresh ginger root, finely chopped

4 fresh green chillies, finely chopped

1 teaspoon turmeric powder

1 teaspoon chilli powder

2 onions, finely sliced

50g/2 oz frozen green peas, defrosted

salt

Peel the potatoes and cut them into small cubes. In a medium saucepan, boil the potatoes in a generous quantity of water until tender. Drain and mash them.

Meanwhile, in another saucepan, boil the black eye and mung beans together in some water for 20 minutes until the beans are cooked. Drain the water and set the beans aside.

Heat the oil in a large saucepan. Add the mustard seeds and, as they begin to pop, add the curry leaves, ginger, green chilli, turmeric and chilli powder and some salt. Stir in the onions and cook, stirring occasionally, for 10 minutes or until the onions are almost brown.

Add the beans, potatoes and peas and mix carefully. When thoroughly combined, set the filling mixture aside while you make the dosa.

Cook the dosa as per the recipe opposite and fill as instructed.

Mushroom and cashew nut samosas

Samosas are well-known in Britain and other Western countries but in Kerala, they are rather new and found only in bakeries or at special functions. Filling the samosas with mushrooms, crunchy cashews and Keralan spices such as mustard seeds and curry leaves is an idea we developed at Rasa. Potatoes and garam masala is the filling most commonly used in North India. I recommend serving a fresh tomato chutney with these samosas and, because they are so light, I find I can easily consume three or four with my afternoon tea.

serves 4

3 tablespoons oil, plus extra for deep-frying
1 teaspoon mustard seeds
2 medium onions, finely sliced
a few curry leaves
1/2 teaspoon turmeric powder
1/4 teaspoon chilli powder
1/4 teaspoon garam masala
75g/3 oz cashew nuts, chopped
2 potatoes, diced
200g/7 oz mushrooms, finely sliced
1 carrot, diced
250g/9 oz ready-made samosa pastry
salt

Heat 3 tablespoons of oil in a large frying pan. Add the mustard seeds and, as they begin to pop, add the onions and curry leaves and cook for 5 minutes over a medium heat until the onions are soft.

Mix in the turmeric, chilli powder, garam masala and some salt, then add the cashew nuts and stir well. Cover and cook for 3 minutes.

Add the potatoes, mushrooms and carrot and cook for 15 to 20 minutes, stirring frequently, until the vegetables are tender. Remove the pan from the heat and set aside to cool.

Fold each sheet of pastry in half lengthways to give 2 layers, then cut into strips measuring about 30cm/12 in x 5.5cm/3 in.

Place a tablespoon of the vegetable mixture in the middle at the end of one pastry strip. Fold a corner of the pastry over the mixture to form a triangle and continue folding in alternate directions until you have a triangular parcel. Repeat with the remaining pastry and filling.

Heat a generous quantity of oil in a deep-fryer, wok or large, heavy saucepan. When the oil is hot, gently place a samosa in the oil and fry until golden brown. Remove and drain on kitchen paper, then repeat with the remaining samosas. Serve hot or cold.

Cassava chips

In Kerala, cassava (also known as tapioca) is grown throughout the year. Housewives prepare them in large quantities for daily teatime snacks. The chips made from them are similar to the potato chips sold widely in Western countries and can be served simply salted or, as in this recipe, seasoned with spices. If you like, use a sharp slicer or mandolin to finely slice the cassava then fry to give cassava crisps. Another variation is to simply boil the cassava and serve it plain with chutneys.

serves 4

3 large cassavas
1/2 teaspoon turmeric powder
a few curry leaves, finely chopped
1 teaspoon chilli powder
vegetable oil, for deep-frying
salt

Peel the cassavas and slice the flesh very finely. Place in a large bowl and gently mix in the turmeric, curry leaves, chilli and some salt to taste.

Heat some oil in a deep-fryer, wok or large, heavy saucepan. Working in small batches, fry the cassava for 2 to 3 minutes until the chips float to the surface.

Use a slotted spoon to remove the chips from the oil and drain them on kitchen paper. Continue until all the cassava is used.

Allow the chips to cool, then store them in an airtight container.

Potato and coriander vadai

Fresh coriander and potato is a very refreshing combination, but not one traditional in Kerala where we tend to prefer yam and cassava. This delicious savoury snack comes from the North of India and Bombay. It is cooked in front of your eyes on nearly every street corner. Just as South Indian food is gaining popularity in the North, their food – and especially this snack – is increasingly popular in the South.

serves 4

2 medium potatoes
500g/1 lb 2 oz chickpea flour
2 tablespoons coriander leaves, chopped
1 fresh green chilli, chopped
1 tablespoon turmeric powder
a pinch of asafoetida
vegetable oil, for deep-frying
salt

Slice the potatoes into 1.5cm/3/4 in rounds. Soak them in a bowl of water with 2 tablespoons of salt.

Place the chickpea flour, coriander, chilli, turmeric and asafoetida in a large bowl and mix well. Stir in 450ml/16 fl oz of water, or just enough to give a thin batter.

Heat the oil in a deep-fryer, wok or large, heavy saucepan. Pat dry the potato slices and dip them in the batter to coat completely.

Fry the coated potato slices one at a time for 2 to 3 minutes or until golden. Remove from the oil and drain on kitchen paper. Serve immediately.

Medhu vadai

Vadais are South India's great treats, a popular snack on Indian trains and an important daily item in my father's teashop. The word vadai is literally translated as 'soft, silky dumplings' but in fact they have a spongy interior and crunchy case. This snack, made from urad dal and spices, can be obtained in any South Indian restaurant. Serve them with coconut and tamarind chutney *(see page 38).*

serves 4

400g/14 oz urad dal
1 onion, finely chopped
2 fresh green chillies, finely chopped
2.5cm/1 in cube fresh ginger, peeled and finely chopped
10 curry leaves, finely chopped
vegetable oil, for deep-frying
salt

Place the dal in a bowl, cover with water and soak for 1 hour. Drain thoroughly and grind the dal in a blender for 10 minutes until the texture is smooth.

Transfer the dal to a large bowl and add the onion, chillies, ginger, curry leaves and a little salt. Mix thoroughly.

Heat the oil in a deep-fryer, wok or large, heavy saucepan. Take golfball-sized pieces of the mixture. Roll and flatten them slightly, then make a hole in the centre.

Place the vadai in the oil a few at a time and fry for 5 minutes or until deep golden brown. Remove and drain on kitchen paper.

curry leaves

Pal katti porichattu

Cheese making is part of North India's food culture, where they have many milk products in their diet. This is not the case in the South because milk is very expensive, and a great deal of it is required to make even a small amount of paneer cheese or pal katti. However, as Northern food becomes more popular in the South, nearly all restaurants are serving paneer dishes and, for Kerala's vegetarians, the cheese is a useful addition to the diet. This particular recipe for cheese dipped in spicy batter is typical of home-style rather than restaurant cooking but could be described as a rich man's snack or one served only on special occasions as paneer is too pricey to eat on a daily basis. Serve it with tomato chutney *(see page 41).*

serves 4
50g/2 oz rice flour
50g/2 oz gram flour
1 fresh green chilli, chopped
10 curry leaves, finely chopped
1 teaspoon black sesame seeds
¹/₂ teaspoon chilli powder
a pinch of turmeric powder
100g/3¹/₂ oz paneer
vegetable oil, for deep-frying
salt

Place the flours, green chilli, curry leaves, sesame seeds, chilli powder, turmeric and a little salt in a large bowl and mix well. Stir in 570ml/1 pint of water, or just enough to give a smooth batter. Whisk until thoroughly blended and smooth, then set the batter aside for 5 minutes.

Cut the cheese into 1cm/¹/₂ in cubes. Heat the oil in a deep-fryer, wok or large, heavy saucepan. Place the pieces of cheese in the batter and stir to coat completely.

Fry the coated cheese one piece at a time in the hot oil for 2 to 3 minutes until golden. Remove from the oil, drain on kitchen paper and serve immediately.

Mixed vegetable pakoda

I got this recipe several years ago from my sister. It's perfect for vegetarians and made from a nutritious mixture of gram flour and spices. The main ingredients here are cauliflower, aubergine and onion, but other vegetables can be used instead. The pakoda go well with tomato chutney (see page 41).

serves 4

100g/3½ oz gram flour
50g/2 oz coriander leaves, finely chopped
1cm/½ in ginger, finely chopped
½ teaspoon chilli powder
½ teaspoon turmeric powder
50g/2 oz aubergine, finely sliced
50g/2 oz cauliflower, cut into florets
1 onion, sliced into rings
vegetable oil, for deep-frying
salt

Place the gram flour, coriander, ginger, chilli, turmeric and salt to taste in a large bowl and mix well. Stir in 570ml/1 pint of water, or just enough to give a smooth batter. Whisk until thoroughly blended and smooth, then set aside for 5 minutes.

Heat the oil in a deep-fryer, wok or large, heavy saucepan. Dip the cut vegetables in the batter to coat completely.

Fry the coated vegetables one at a time for 2 to 3 minutes or until golden. Remove from the oil and drain on kitchen paper. Serve immediately.

Koonu bhajia

Battered and fried vegetable snacks, such as these crunchy mushrooms, are common all over India. They can be made with most vegetables. Onion and potato bhajia are the most common but mushroom makes a pleasant change. This dish (one of the simplest in the book) is my own idea – in Kerala, mushrooms tend to be used only in curries and thorans.

serves 4

150g/5 oz mushrooms
300g/10½ oz rice flour
½ teaspoon turmeric powder
½ teaspoon chilli powder
a few sprigs of fresh coriander, finely chopped
vegetable oil, for deep-frying
salt

Halve the mushrooms. In a mixing bowl, combine the rice flour, turmeric, chilli powder, coriander and some salt. Stir in about 225ml/8 fl oz of water or just enough to make a thick batter.

Heat the oil in a deep-fryer, wok or large, heavy saucepan. Dip the mushrooms in the batter and fry until golden brown and crisp. Allow them to cool before serving.

Rasa idli

In South India, idli is usually served during breakfast and accompanied by sambar and coconut chutney. North Indian people tend to like our idlies as much as they do our dosas and make them just as regularly. For my restaurants I have created this snack version which incorporates a vegetable masala to give a unique taste. It's my favourite tiffin and, if you ask anyone from North India what their favourite Southern dish is, they will quite possibly say idlies too.

serves 4

295g/10½ oz long-grain rice

75g/3 oz urad dal

vegetable oil, for greasing

curry leaves, to decorate (optional)

salt

for the masala:

2 tablespoons vegetable oil

1 teaspoon mustard seeds

50g/2 oz onions

1 teaspoon ground coriander

½ teaspoon chilli powder

½ teaspoon turmeric powder

30g/1 oz tomatoes

40g/1½ oz peas

1 teaspoon ground pepper, or to taste

In a large bowl, soak the rice for at least 8 hours in a generous quantity of water. At the same time, in a separate bowl, soak the urad dal.

Drain the rice and dal, keeping them separate. Place the rice in a blender and grind for 5 minutes, slowly adding 120ml/4 fl oz of water to give a smooth paste. Transfer the paste to a large bowl.

Rinse out the blender, and then grind the urad dal for 5 minutes, slowly adding 4 tablespoons of water to make a paste. Add the dal paste to the bowl of rice paste and mix well. Stir in some salt, then cover the bowl with a damp cloth and leave to ferment for 8 hours, during which time the batter will increase in volume and become a mass of small bubbles.

To make the masala, heat the oil in a large saucepan. Add the mustard seeds and, as they begin to pop, add the onions and a little salt and cook until soft.

Add the coriander, chilli and turmeric. Mix well, then add the tomatoes and 4 tablespoons of water and cook for 2 minutes.

Stir in the peas and pepper. Cover the pan and cook for 15 minutes or until the peas are tender. Remove from the heat.

Prepare a steamer with water and bring to the boil. Smear the idli moulds with a little oil. Pour a spoonful of the masala in each mould and top with the idli batter. Place the moulds in the steamer and top with a curry leaf, if using. Cover and cook for 7 to 10 minutes. Serve hot with coconut chutney *(see page 38).*

Rava cake

My sister Padmini likes to prepare this sweet semolina dish for afternoon snacks. It reminds me of vattayappam, a traditional rice cake made from palm sugar, but using semolina gives a softer and lighter texture. If you are not familiar with semolina, do not worry – it is very easy to use. This cake can be eaten on its own but also goes well with mango or coconut chutney.

serves 4

185g/6$^{1}/_{2}$ oz semolina
1 tablespoon ghee or butter
225ml/8 fl oz milk
60g/2$^{1}/_{2}$ oz grated jaggery
100g/3$^{1}/_{2}$ oz freshly grated or desiccated coconut
8 cardamom pods
$^{1}/_{4}$ teaspoon baking soda

Place a large, heavy saucepan over a medium heat and toast the semolina for 5 minutes, stirring continuously, until the grains turn golden. Add the ghee or butter and keep stirring to prevent lumps.

When the ghee is combined, mix in all the other ingredients, stirring continuously. Remove from the direct heat and keep warm.

Cut a few slits in some greaseproof paper and oil it lightly. Use this to line a steamer and set it over simmering water.

Pour the semolina mixture onto the paper. Cover and cook for 10 to 15 minutes until firm. Remove and cut into diamond shapes. Serve hot.

cardamom pods

Semiya uppuma

Uppuma is a very popular breakfast dish in South India and this snack flavoured with chilli and ginger is made in the same way. You could also serve it as an alternative to rice at main meals. It's light and refreshing and, unlike rice, can be prepared in less than five minutes. Customers at our restaurants love it.

serves 4

3 tablespoons ghee
200g/7 oz fine vermicelli
1 teaspoon mustard seeds
1 teaspoon urad dal
10 curry leaves
25g/1 oz cashew nuts
1 onion, finely chopped
3 fresh green chillies, finely chopped
2.5cm/1 in fresh root ginger, peeled and finely chopped
a pinch of turmeric powder
salt

Heat the ghee in a large wok or frying pan over a medium heat. When hot, add the vermicelli and stir-fry for 5 to 6 minutes or until golden brown. Use a slotted spoon to remove the vermicelli from the pan and set aside to drain on kitchen paper.

Add the mustard seeds to the pan and, as they begin to pop, add the urad dal, curry leaves and cashews. Sauté until the nuts are brown. Add the onion, chillies and ginger and cook, stirring, for 5 minutes or until the onion softens.

Stir in the turmeric, season to taste with salt, then pour in 570ml/1 pint of water and bring to the boil. Lower the heat, add the vermicelli and continue cooking for another 3 to 4 minutes until the vermicelli is thoroughly combined with the spices. Serve hot.

chutneys and pickles

Keralan mothers take particular pride in their fresh chutneys and pickles. They are, I think, the most memorable element of a home-cooked meal, giving each one an unmistakable, strong and refreshing flavour. I don't remember a day on which we didn't have chutney with our lunch. Often no elaborate cooking was involved, but there would definitely be a special chutney or a good pickle offered along with fresh, home-made yogurt.

My mum's tender mango and gooseberry pickles are very famous in our village and no meals were complete without them as far as we were concerned. Anybody who visited our home would get a small present of a beautiful bottle of tiny whole mangoes bobbing in hot red chilli sauce. In the mango season, we would preserve the fruit in large Chinese clay jars filled with salt, then use them during the monsoon when nothing happens in Kerala except heavy rain.

Kerala's best-known pickles are tender mango, cut mango, gooseberry, lime and lemon. People are often not fond of lime or lemon pickles because of their strong sour taste but I love them equally well and they are very easy to make.

Chutneys have great importance in our everyday lives. They are much more than a mere accompaniment to crisp snacks and feature prominently in main meals. We even start the day with them – at breakfast fresh coconut chutney is served alongside pancakes and steamed cakes like idlies. When I first came to Britain, I was astonished to find that pickles and chutneys were only served as a 'first course' with poppadoms. And I was concerned that most of the restaurants didn't prepare their own pickles and chutneys. They still don't – buying them in bulk from the cash-and-carry instead. To me it is wrong and inauthentic: if chefs don't make their own pickles on the premises, it would be like my mum borrowing the neighbour's pickles for our family meals.

I wanted to do things differently and my intention when opening Rasa was to create a new reputation for poppadoms and pickles. They are the first thing to come to the dinner table, and as such are an important item with which to be creative and impress the guests. To that end, we serve them with the varied crisp and crunchy snacks many people had not seen before Rasa opened. I like to think that by doing this, in Britain at least, we gave birth to fresh chutneys and pickles.

Coconut and tamarind chutney

Dosa and coconut chutney is like bread and butter to South Indian people and, in my opinion, the best chutneys are made with coconut. In this recipe, tamarind pulp and extra spices are added to Kerala's basic fresh coconut chutney, giving a stronger, more pungent flavour. It goes very well with dosas, of course, but my favourite way to serve it is with lots of freshly made Rasa idlies *(see page 32).*

serves 4

2 teaspoons tamarind pulp

125g/4$^{1}/_{2}$ oz freshly grated coconut

3 fresh green chillies

1 tablespoon finely chopped root ginger

1 teaspoon finely chopped garlic

2 tablespoons vegetable oil

$^{1}/_{2}$ teaspoon mustard seeds

1 teaspoon urad dal

3 dried red chillies

10 curry leaves

salt

Place the tamarind pulp in a bowl with 1 tablespoon of hot water and break up the tamarind as much as possible with a spoon. Set aside for 20 to 30 minutes, stirring occasionally to dissolve the pulp as much as possible. Sieve the mixture to give 1 tablespoon of thick tamarind-flavoured liquid.

In a grinder or blender, process the tamarind liquid, coconut, fresh green chillies, ginger, garlic and a little salt to give a fine paste. Transfer the mixture to a bowl.

Heat the oil in a frying pan over a medium heat. Add the mustard seeds and, as they begin to pop, add the urad dal, dried red chillies and curry leaves. Stir-fry until the dal turns golden.

Pour the contents of the pan over the coconut mixture and stir well before serving.

Mulagu chutney

This bell pepper chutney came about one day when I was experimenting in the kitchen. I was fascinated with the peppers' colour and texture. They reminded me of the chilli chutney that my sister used to make, and for which she was famous locally. For me, this variation has a better flavour because of the refreshing sweetness of the pepper. Serve it as an accompaniment to rice and curry dishes.

serves 4

5 tablespoons tamarind pulp

5 tablespoons vegetable oil

1 teaspoon mustard seeds

1 teaspoon urad dal

5 curry leaves

a pinch of turmeric powder

a pinch of asafoetida

a pinch of fenugreek seeds

2 red bell peppers, chopped

2 green bell peppers, chopped

2 fresh green chillies, chopped

6 cloves garlic, sliced

salt

In a small saucepan, heat 225ml/8 fl oz of water until piping hot. Turn off the heat and add the tamarind, breaking it into pieces. Soak for 20 to 30 minutes, stirring occasionally to help dissolve the pulp as much as possible. Sieve the mixture to give a thin tamarind-flavoured liquid. Set aside.

Heat 1 tablespoon of the oil in a wok or kadai. Add the mustard seeds and, when they begin to pop, add the urad dal, curry leaves, turmeric, asafoetida and fenugreek. Cook over a low heat, stirring occasionally, until the urad dal is browned. Remove from the heat and drain off the oil, reserving it. Transfer the spice mixture to a plate and set aside.

Heat the remaining fresh oil in the wok. Add the bell peppers, chillies and garlic and cook, stirring, over a low heat for around 10 minutes or until the garlic is golden. Remove from the heat and leave to cool.

Place the spice mixture in a blender and grind for 1 minute. Add the cooked pepper mixture, tamarind liquid and salt to taste. Grind to a coarse (rather than smooth) paste. Then mix in the reserved cooking oil.

Transfer the chutney to a serving bowl, or store in a screw-top jar in the refrigerator for up to 1 week.

Aubergine chutney

Hyderabad is the chutney capital of India. No meal there is complete without a selection of chutneys and dry chutney powders, which are moistened with ghee or oil before serving to give a fresh feel. They like their condiments hot, too, in that area and many of them can be stored for a very long time. This delightful dish from the princely houses of Hyderabad can be eaten with bread and rice or even as a sandwich spread. The smoky flavour of the cooked aubergine really complements the fresh flavours of the spices. In India, people make aubergine chutney in many ways – I like to fry rather than bake the aubergines before grinding.

serves 4

1 tablespoon tamarind pulp
1 aubergine, about 150g/5 oz, diced
4 dried red chillies
1 teaspoon coriander seeds
120ml/4 fl oz vegetable oil
2 teaspoons mustard seeds
5 curry leaves
a pinch of fenugreek seeds
salt

In a small bowl, combine the tamarind in 4 tablespoons of hot water. Break it up as much as possible with a spoon then set aside to dissolve for 20 to 30 minutes.

Meanwhile, soak the diced aubergine in a bowl of cold salted water for 5 minutes. Drain and pat dry with kitchen paper.

Place the chillies and coriander in a dry frying pan and toast for 2 to 3 minutes over a medium heat until fragrant. Remove from the pan and set aside.

Sieve the dissolved tamarind to extract the seeds and give 4 tablespoons of tamarind-flavoured liquid.

Heat 100ml/3½ fl oz of the oil in a medium frying pan over a medium heat. Fry the aubergine until golden brown and soft, then drain on kitchen paper. Wipe the pan clean.

Using a blender, grind together the cooked aubergine, toasted chillies and coriander, tamarind liquid and some salt to give a smooth paste.

Heat another 4 teaspoons of oil in the frying pan. Add the mustard seeds and, as they begin to pop, add the curry leaves and fenugreek. Pour the contents of the pan over the aubergine sauce and stir gently before serving.

Tomato chutney

When an English friend visited our home some years ago, he was surprised that we ate many of our tea-time snacks on their own. He suggested we serve them with a nice fresh dip, so I developed this quick and easy tomato chutney, a fantastic combination of tomatoes and aromatic spices. The result is very much like a Mexican salsa but has more kick. It is best enjoyed with potato and coriander vadai *(see page 28)* or mixed vegetable pakoda *(see page 31)*.

serves 4

4 tomatoes

2 fresh green chillies

2 cloves garlic

**a few fresh coriander leaves, finely chopped
   (optional)**

salt

Place the tomatoes, chillies and garlic in a blender with 1 to 2 tablespoons of water and a little salt. Blend just until the tomatoes are crushed. Place in a serving dish and sprinkle with the coriander leaves, if using.

Mango and yogurt chutney

Mango chutney is the most common type found in Indian restaurants. In terms of flavour and texture, however, this one is quite different. It could be described as a cross between lassi and chutney and is served in bowls alongside the main meal. In this version I have added freshly grated coconut and red chillies to enhance the flavour. The result is spicier and more refreshing than other chutneys – that is how we like them in South India. We often have this for lunch, made from nice homemade yogurt and sweet locally grown mangoes. It goes well with snacks such as Rava cake *(see page 34)*.

serves 4

200g/7 oz sweet mangoes

150g/5 oz plain yogurt

100g/3$\frac{1}{2}$ oz freshly grated or desiccated coconut

1 tablespoon salt

4 dried red chillies

2 teaspoons chilli powder

1 teaspoon fenugreek seeds

Place all the ingredients in a blender and process for 5 minutes or until smooth. Transfer the mixture to an airtight container or screw-top jar and store in the refrigerator for up to 4 days.

Red pepper chutney

I developed this sweet-flavoured chutney for Rasa restaurants. Although not a traditional recipe, it is very moreish – once you start eating it, you cannot stop. It is hotter and much easier to make than the Mulagu chutney *(see page 39)* which is also made from bell peppers. Because this one is very finely ground, it is a better choice for crisp snacks.

serves 4

1 tablespoon tamarind pulp

4 dried red chillies

1 teaspoon coriander seeds

4 red bell peppers, diced

2 tablespoons vegetable oil

2 teaspoons mustard seeds

5 curry leaves

a pinch of fenugreek seeds

salt

In a small bowl, cover the tamarind pulp with 4 tablespoons of hot water. Break up the pulp as much as possible using a small spoon, then leave to soak for 20 to 30 minutes. Sieve to give 4 table-spoons of tamarind water.

Meanwhile, place the chillies and coriander in a dry frying pan and toast for 2 to 3 minutes over a medium heat.

Transfer the toasted spices to a blender and add the bell peppers, tamarind water and some salt. Grind to a smooth paste and transfer to a serving dish.

Heat the oil in a saucepan. Add the mustard seeds and, as they begin to pop, add the curry leaves and fenugreek. Pour the contents of the pan over the red bell pepper mixture and gently stir through before serving.

clockwise from the top: carrot and ginger pickle (page 44), tomato chutney (page 41), red pepper chutney, and mango and yogurt chutney (page 41)

Carrot and ginger pickle

The main ingredients and seasonings of Indian chutneys and pickles vary throughout the country according to the culinary idiosyncrasies of each state, and what is in season. Ginger is grown in Kerala and exported in vast quantities, so naturally we use it in pickles and chutneys. This exquisitely flavoured recipe is served at marriages and traditional banquets.

serves 4

75g/3 oz tamarind pulp
100g/3¹/₂ oz carrots
100g/3¹/₂ oz root ginger, peeled
50g/1³/₄ oz garlic cloves, finely chopped
5 tablespoons vegetable oil
1 teaspoon mustard seeds
1 teaspoon urad dal
10 curry leaves
8 fresh green chillies, halved
50g/1³/₄ oz jaggery
1 teaspoon turmeric powder
salt

In a small saucepan, bring 100ml/3¹/₂ fl oz of water to boil. Add the tamarind pulp and simmer gently for 20 minutes or until the water thickens, stirring occasionally. Meanwhile, cut the carrots and ginger into 2.5cm/1 in strips and chop the garlic finely.

When the tamarind mixture is ready, remove it from the heat and sieve into a bowl to remove the seeds and skin. Set aside.

Heat the oil in a kadai or wok. Add the mustard seeds and, as they begin to pop, add the urad dal and curry leaves. Cook, stirring frequently, until the urad dal turns brown.

Add the carrots, ginger, garlic and chillies to the pan and sauté for 2 minutes. Add the jaggery, turmeric and some salt to taste and sauté for another 2 minutes. Then pour in the tamarind liquid and simmer over a medium heat for 10 minutes until the vegetables are cooked and the sauce is thick.

Remove the mixture from the heat and leave to cool. Store in an airtight container or screw-top jar for up to 7 days.

Chilli and ginger pickle

One of the simplest recipes I have created for Rasa restaurants, this pickle is my wife's favourite. It can be eaten with any bread or rice dish. Alison likes me to fry the ginger for a while before adding the chillies so that the ginger is browned and crisp rather than raw-tasting. In India the Brahmins make a similar pickle but add tamarind liquid instead of vinegar – a good variation for you to try. The chillies correctly used here are not the normal large green chillies used in the other recipes in this book, but smaller ones shaped like bullets.

serves 4

8 tablespoons vegetable oil

1 teaspoon mustard seeds

1 teaspoon turmeric

250g/9 oz fresh green bullet chillies, slit lengthways

200g/7 oz root ginger, finely sliced

350ml/12½ fl oz white vinegar

a pinch of asafoetida

salt

Heat the oil in a large frying pan. Add the mustard seeds and, as they begin to pop, add the turmeric, salt, green chillies and ginger. Cook over a medium heat for 10 minutes, stirring frequently.

Lower the heat and add the vinegar. Cook for 5 minutes or until the mixture is a little drier.

Add the asafoetida and stir well. Remove the pan from the heat and set aside to cool. Transfer the pickle to a screw-top jar and store in the fridge, where it will keep for around 2 weeks.

Inji pachadi

The most common pickle in Keralan homes, this pungent mixture is sweet, sour and hot but mellow at the same time. We use yogurt in most of our meals in one way or another. This kind of creamy chutney goes particularly well with mild dishes because it helps enhance their flavour, but can be served with any curry. It also makes a superb dip and is quite delicious with breads, especially paratha *(see pages 49–50)*.

serves 4

5cm/2 in piece root ginger, peeled and chopped

1 teaspoon freshly grated or desiccated coconut

225g/8 oz plain yogurt

½ teaspoon sugar

1 tablespoon vegetable oil

½ teaspoon mustard seeds

5 curry leaves

a pinch of asafoetida

salt

Place the ginger and coconut in a grinder and grind to a fine paste. In a medium bowl, whisk the yogurt until smooth, then add the ginger paste, sugar and some salt.

Heat the oil in a small saucepan. Add the mustard seeds and, as they begin to pop, stir in the curry leaves and asafoetida. Pour the contents of the pan over the yogurt mixture and serve cold.

breads and rice

breads

The Southern Indian diet is traditionally rice based. Whether eating at home or at a function, we always want to have rice and curry dishes. Recent years, however, have seen an increasingly diverse approach to meals and Keralans have started including more bread in their diet, not least because our doctors are recommending we eat wholemeal bread once a day for health. The bread recipes we are now using exhibit a variety of cultural influences.

The situation in North India has traditionally been quite the opposite. They eat breads all the time. When dining in restaurants in Delhi, I have always enjoyed their wide variety of breads such as tandoor paratha, nan and dry chapattis, with excellent dal and chickpea dishes. In the North, paratha, which is a comparatively thick flatbread, and the thinner roti, are made on hot griddles and cooked with a lot of ghee. The style is comparatively heavy, so when Keralans make these breads we tend to apply very little ghee or, most of the time, none at all.

I think South India now offers a wider variety and more unusual flavours of bread than the North. Appams and idiappams, for example, are very light and sweet and flavoured with fresh coconut. My favourite is idiappam, which is made from steamed rice vermicelli and goes very well with a mixed vegetable and coconut stew. Kerala's best-known bread, however, is the Malabar paratha, a wonderfully layered Muslim speciality from the northern part of the state, but popular all over South India. When eating an old-fashioned thali – a large, round food platter featuring lots of small dishes – chapatti is a must, but it is also popular with a simple vegetable korma.

Kerala paratha

My favourite bread for everyday eating, the Kerala paratha is lighter and flakier than North Indian parathas. In other parts of India they tend to stuff their parathas with a variety of ingredients, including fish, meat and vegetables. Normally Keralans eat this bread with dry dishes such as thoran, spinach and baby potatoes, and chickpea dishes. However, when there is not much time to cook, we also like to eat it in the North Indian manner, served simply with a pickle, which we always have in the kitchen.

serves 4

225g/8 oz wholemeal flour, plus extra for dusting
4 tablespoons vegetable oil, plus extra
   for greasing

Place the flour in a mixing bowl. Gradually add the oil and 150ml/5 fl oz of water to give a soft, pliable dough. Knead for a few minutes, then set aside to rest for 1 hour.

Divide the dough into 8 equal portions. Place one piece in the palm of your hand and roll it into a smooth ball. Lightly coat it with flour, then place on a board and roll out to a 15cm/6 in round.

Smear the surface of the rolled dough with a thin layer of oil. Starting at the end nearest to you, roll the dough over and over to give a long sausage shape.

Carefully lift up the roll and place one end of it in the centre of your palm. Wind the rest of the roll around this centre point to give a circle and flatten the circle between your palms.

Coat the circle of dough with dry flour and carefully roll it out into a round no larger than 12.5cm/5 in.

Heat a griddle and, when hot, place the paratha on it. Sprinkle a little oil around the paratha and cook, turning frequently, until the paratha is golden brown on both sides.

Vegetable paratha

A variation of the traditional Kerala paratha *(see page 49)*, this bread is nevertheless reminiscent of North India's stuffed parathas. It adds variety to mealtimes and, as the vegetables are already in the paratha, one can make fewer curries. It can be served as a snack or light lunch, served with a simple coconut or coriander chutney.

serves 4

400g/14 oz wholemeal flour, plus extra
for dusting

3 tablespoons vegetable oil, plus extra
for greasing

salt

for the masala:

4 tablespoons vegetable oil

1 teaspoon mustard seeds

10 curry leaves

1 teaspoon urad dal

2 fresh green chillies, finely chopped

2 cloves garlic, finely chopped

2.5cm/1 in piece fresh ginger, finely chopped

2 onions, finely sliced

1 teaspoon garam masala

¼ teaspoon turmeric powder

¼ teaspoon chilli powder

¼ teaspoon ground coriander

1 tomato, chopped

1 red bell pepper, chopped

100g/3½ oz potato, chopped

100g/3½ oz cauliflower, chopped

2 eggs

In a large mixing bowl, place the flour, a little salt and the oil. Slowly mix in 570ml/1 pint of water to give a smooth dough. Cover with a cloth and set aside for 20 minutes.

To make the masala, heat the oil in a large frying pan. Add the mustard seeds and, when they begin to pop, add the curry leaves and urad dal. Cook for 2 minutes until the urad dal turns brown.

Add the green chillies, garlic and ginger and sauté for 2 minutes. Stir in the onions and cook, stirring regularly, for a further 5 minutes until the onion turns soft.

Mix in the garam masala, turmeric, chilli powder, coriander and tomato and cook for 2 minutes.

Add the bell pepper, potato, cauliflower and some salt and cook the mixture for a further 5 minutes over a low heat until the vegetables are tender. Remove from the heat and set aside to cool.

Beat the eggs in a large bowl. When the vegetable mixture is cold, combine it with the eggs.

Divide the dough into 8 equal portions. Place one piece in the palm of your hand and roll it into a smooth ball. Lightly coat it with flour, then place on a board and roll out to a 15cm/6 in round. Smear it with a thin layer of oil.

Heat the griddle, then place the piece of rolled dough on it. Sprinkle some oil around the paratha, then spread 3 tablespoons of the masala mixture over the top. When the bottom is cooked, turn the paratha over carefully, add a little more oil and cook for 1 minute until the egg and vegetable mixture turns brown.

Repeat the process with the rest of the dough and masala. Serve hot.

Onion chapatti

The people from North India and Bombay introduced chapattis to the South of the country and, in general, we Keralans now prefer them to rice at dinnertime. Chapattis are the staple of the Punjabi diet, simple flat wholewheat breads that can be stuffed with many different ingredients. Potatoes are the best-known filling and the result is served as aloo paratha in many British curry houses. In North India, it is fashionable to make chapattis flavoured with things like fenugreek leaves or sesame seeds. Chapattis can be served at any Indian meal, but are especially good alongside vegetarian dishes.

400g/14 oz wholemeal flour, plus extra for dusting
2 teaspoons vegetable oil
10 shallots, finely chopped
1 teaspoon cumin seeds
salt

Place the flour, oil and a pinch of salt in a mixing bowl. Slowly add 200ml/7 fl oz of water, then the shallots and cumin and mix to a smooth dough. Leave to stand for 10 minutes.

On a floured work surface, knead the dough for about 3 minutes. Take golfball-sized pieces of the dough and roll them out as thinly as possible, turning the chapatti frequently to give an even, round shape.

Heat a griddle (without using any oil) and, when hot, place a chapatti on the surface. Cook, turning frequently, until done. Remove from the griddle and serve immediately. Repeat with the remaining dough.

Idiappam

Our favourite breakfast during childhood, these very light, coconut-flavoured rice noodle cakes were the only dish we could eat every day without complaint. Normally we would have them with a chickpea curry or potato stew. I remember we kids all had different likes when it came to food, and had a habit of showing our dissatisfaction – the only thing we all loved was idiappam. They come from the same family as idli and sannas. At supper-time, serve them with kadala curry, vegetable korma or sambar.

serves 4

400g/14oz rice flour
570ml/1 pint milk
a pinch of salt
100g/3½ oz freshly grated coconut

Put the rice flour in a kadai or wok and toast for 5 minutes until the colour turns light brown.

In a saucepan, heat the milk and, when hot, pour it onto the rice flour. Add the salt and mix slowly to make a dough.

Heat the idli steamer. Take small balls of the dough and push them through the idiappam press. Add the fresh coconut to the idli moulds. Press the dough to make a heap of rice noodles and top it with fresh coconut. Repeat with the rest of the dough and coconut.

Steam the idiappam for 5 minutes before serving with curry.

Sannas

Sannas are similar to English dumplings but have a slightly bubblier texture, not unlike that of appam. At breakfast time in North Kerala they are eaten with coconut chutney as an accompaniment to leftover wet curries, but in the Christian community of Mangalore City, where sannas originated, they are normally eaten with a pork dish. I have enjoyed them many times with vegetable korma when visiting the area. We don't make them on a daily basis for Rasa restaurants, but offer them on special occasion menus such as on Valentine's Day.

serves 4

100g/3½ oz basmati rice
50g/1¾ oz urad dal
3 tablespoons sugar
1 teaspoon dried yeast
salt

In a large bowl, soak the rice and dal for at least 3 hours in a generous quantity of water.

Drain the rice and dal, then place them in a blender. Grind for 5 minutes, slowly adding 120ml/4 fl oz of water to give a smooth paste. Transfer the paste to a large bowl.

Stir in the sugar, yeast and some salt. Leave to ferment for 2 hours, during which time the batter will increase in volume and become a mass of small bubbles.

Prepare a steamer with boiling water. Smear some idli moulds with a little oil. Pour a spoonful of the batter into each mould and cook covered in the steamer for 7 to 10 minutes. Remove and serve hot with coconut chutney *(see page 38)*.

Mutta appam

Appam is a Keralan Christian dish and an Easter speciality, enjoyed after the fasting period. This egg-filled variation is a modern version of the dish that is popular with Kerala's many experimental cooks, but it is also famous in Sri Lanka where it is known as egg hoppers. Mutta appam goes well with lightly spiced vegetable stews and kormas, and can be eaten for breakfast on its own or with a pickle such as coconut chutney.

serves 4–6

250g/9oz basmati rice
125g/4½ oz freshly grated or desiccated coconut
1 teaspoon sugar
1 teaspoon dried yeast
75g/3 oz semolina
1 teaspoon salt
4–6 eggs (optional)
vegetable oil, for frying

Wash the rice in cold water, then transfer it to a bowl and cover with 500ml/18 fl oz of fresh water. Leave to soak for 1 hour. Drain, reserving 225ml/8 fl oz of the soaking water. Transfer the rice and reserved water to a grinder or blender. Add the coconut and grind until fine. Set the mixture aside.

Place 5 teaspoons of lukewarm water in a small bowl. Add the sugar, stir to dissolve, then add the yeast. Cover the bowl with clingfilm and set aside.

Place the semolina in a saucepan with 150ml/5 fl oz of water. Place over a medium heat and cook for about 15 minutes, stirring occasionally, until thick. Remove from the heat and place in a large bowl.

Add the ground rice mixture and yeast mixture to the cooked semolina. Stir well and cover with a damp cloth. Leave for at least 4 hours, or until the mixture is bubbly and has doubled in volume.

Add the salt to the batter and stir well, being careful not to knock the air out of the mixture.

Lightly grease a kadai or large non-stick frying pan and place over a medium heat. Add a ladle of the appam mixture to the pan and spread it thinly over the base as though making a crêpe. Cover and cook for 2 minutes.

Remove the lid and crack a whole egg, if using, into the middle of the pan. Cover and cook for a further 2 to 3 minutes, until the base is golden and crisp and the top surface is soft.

Use a spatula to remove the appam from the pan and serve hot with coconut chutney *(see page 38)*. Repeat with the remaining mixture, adding eggs to the appams if desired.

rice dishes

Rice is the staple starch food of Kerala and the rest of South India. During feasts and festivals, it is cooked in huge quantities in the largest pots you are ever likely to see. Rice dishes are the most popular ones served at these big parties and, because the feasts are free, people tend to take the opportunity to eat as much rice as possible. We kids used to find this funny. With thousands of people queuing up to eat at once, it was easy for big-bellied eaters and naughty kids like me to line up twice or sometimes three times in the oottupura or dining hall and eat rice until our stomachs were full.

In Kerala, we have rice at least twice a day for meals and, in addition, rice is used very frequently as an ingredient in breakfast dishes and snacks. Kerala has its own special variety of red rice and in the villages we tend to prefer it to expensive basmati – our rice tastes earthier and is more filling at mealtimes.

Keralan curry dishes are full of intricate flavours and are ideally served with plain rice. I still love to eat that way whenever I am back home. Flavoured rice is served on special occasions, especially the Muslim dish biryani, which is well liked by people of all communities for special functions and feasts. The Brahmin communities in Tamil Nadu and Kerala have also introduced our people to an array of flavoured rice dishes. These include those made with tamarind, lemon or coconut, plus a refreshing yogurt and green chilli rice, which is served cold. They all taste remarkably different and make an attractive, colourful display on the dinner table.

At Rasa we introduced all these unusual rice dishes, giving people more choice than the pilau and plain boiled rice options typically offered in other Indian restaurants in Britain. We find the rice section of the menu intrigues customers and our rice dishes now receive the same attention as the starters and main course curries. Increasingly I find that British people want to eat rice and, sometimes at our restaurants, they will choose to have a rice dish on its own, which – believe it or not – can be quite appealing when the rice is freshly cooked and nicely flavoured in the South Indian manner. All the recipes here are easy to follow and can be made with white basmati rice.

Black pepper rice

Based on a North Indian dish, this is a unique combination of spices and rice in which I have included a few curry leaves and green chillies to alter the taste of the original. Black pepper is indigenous to Kerala and inextricably linked to our history and society. Through agriculture, it is used as a means of making money, but it is also used as a medicine and, of course, Keralan people are passionate about it in food.

serves 4

8 tablespoons vegetable oil

50g/2 oz onions, finely chopped

400g/14 oz basmati rice

2 fresh green chillies, split lengthways

10 curry leaves

1 teaspoon mustard seeds

1 teaspoon cumin seeds

½ teaspoon black peppercorns

1 teaspoon salt

Heat 5 tablespoons of the oil in a wok or frying pan. When the oil is hot, add the onions and fry, stirring frequently, until golden brown. Remove from the pan and set aside to drain.

Wash the rice in several changes of water until the water runs clear. Place in a bowl, then cover with more water to a depth of 2.5cm/1 in. Leave to soak for 30 minutes, then drain.

In a large, heavy saucepan, heat the remaining oil over a medium-high heat. Add the chillies, curry leaves, mustard seeds, cumin and peppercorns. Stir-fry for 10 seconds, then add the rice and salt and stir gently.

Pour 600ml/20 fl oz of water into the saucepan and bring to the boil. Cover tightly, lower the heat right down and cook for 25 minutes. Remove the lid, fluff up the rice with a fork and, before serving, sprinkle with the fried crispy onions.

Bisi bele rice

This recipe, a traditional Brahmin speciality from Karnataka, was given to me by my friend's mother, Mrs Rajagopal, who lives in Mysore. It is a favourite dish of hers, similar to biryani but more moist and made with lentils as well as rice. Like biryani, bisi bele rice is usually served on auspicious occasions. The Brahmins love colourful food like this.

serves 4

50g/2 oz tamarind pulp
150g/5 oz toor dal
4 tablespoons vegetable oil
75g/3 oz freshly grated coconut
7 dried red chillies
2 teaspoons coriander seeds
1 teaspoon chana dal
1 teaspoon urad dal
1 teaspoon turmeric powder
1/2 teaspoon fenugreek seeds
a pinch of asafoetida
500g/1 lb 2 oz basmati rice
1 teaspoon mustard seeds
10 curry leaves
2 tablespoons chopped raw cashew nuts
salt

In a small bowl, cover the tamarind pulp with 120ml/4 fl oz of hot water and break up with a spoon. Leave to soak for 20 to 30 minutes, then sieve the mixture to give 120ml/4 fl oz of tamarind liquid. Discard the seeds and skin.

Meanwhile, place the toor dal in a large saucepan and cover generously with water. Bring to the boil and simmer until the dal is soft. Drain and set aside.

Heat 2 tablespoons of the oil in a frying pan and fry the coconut, chillies, coriander, chana dal, urad dal, turmeric, fenugreek and asafoetida until fragrant. Pour the contents of the pan into a grinder and grind finely.

Wash the rice in cold water and place it in a large pot. Add 1 litre/1 3/4 pints of water and a little salt. Bring to the boil and simmer for about 20 minutes. Add the toor dal, tamarind liquid and the ground spices, plus some salt to taste. Cook for 5 minutes, adding just a little extra hot water if the mixture becomes very dry too quickly.

Heat the remaining oil in a frying pan and add the mustard seeds. As they begin to pop, add the curry leaves and cashew nuts and cook, stirring, until the nuts turn golden brown. Pour the mixture over the cooked rice, mix together and serve hot.

Rasa biryani

A light mixture of spices and vegetables perks up this excellent dish. Biryani is very common in Keralan restaurants but somewhat heavier than our normal rice dishes and is properly served at lunch or dinner with a spicy raita *(see page 124)*. It is a speciality of the Muslim area of North Kerala called Calicut and is well known around the world as a meaty rice dish. In Calicut, biryani is associated with festive cooking and always made with chicken or lamb. This vegetarian version is very popular with our customers.

serves 4

400g/14 oz basmati rice
4 tablespoons oil
10 raw cashew nuts
2 bay leaves
1 cinnamon stick
10 cardamom pods
3 onions, finely sliced
100g/3½ oz carrots, cut into batons
75g/3 oz green beans, trimmed
75g/3 oz peas
75g/3 oz red bell pepper
1 tablespoon chilli powder
1 teaspoon turmeric powder
2cm/¾ in fresh root ginger, finely sliced
1 clove garlic, finely chopped
50g/2 oz ghee
100g/3½ oz broccoli, chopped
75g/3 oz tomatoes, chopped
a few coriander leaves, finely chopped
a few mint leaves, finely chopped
salt

Wash the rice and set aside to drain. In a large saucepan, heat the oil over a medium heat and add the cashews, bay leaves, cinnamon and cardamom. Cook, stirring, for 2 to 3 minutes or until fragrant.

Add the onions and cook for 5 minutes or until the onion is well browned. Mix in the carrots, green beans, peas and red pepper together with the chilli, turmeric, ginger and garlic. Cover and cook for 20 minutes over a very low heat, stirring occasionally.

Meanwhile, in large pan of boiling salted water, cook the rice with the ghee for 20 minutes or until tender. Drain and refresh under cold running water, then set aside to drain thoroughly.

When the vegetables have been cooking for 20 minutes, add the broccoli and tomatoes and continue cooking for 5 minutes.

When the vegetables are cooked, add the cooked rice to the vegetable sauce with some of the coriander and mint and mix well. Transfer to a serving dish, garnish with the remaining herbs and serve hot.

Brinjal rice

Aubergines are much loved all over India. In the villages, whole aubergines are put into hot ashes and left to roast. When they are completely cooked through and quite pulpy inside, the charred skin is removed and the pulp stir-fried with all kinds of spices. This dish from my mother uses more or less the same premise but includes rice.

serves 4

1 tablespoon tamarind pulp
400g/14 oz basmati rice
200g/7 oz baby aubergines
4 tablespoons vegetable oil
1 teaspoon mustard seeds
1 tablespoon black gram dal
3 or 4 curry leaves
4 dried red chillies
2.5cm/1 in stick cinnamon
50g/2 oz freshly grated coconut
1 onion, finely chopped
1 tablespoon lime juice
1/2 teaspoon turmeric powder
1/2 teaspoon chilli powder
a small bunch of fresh coriander leaves, chopped
salt

Place the tamarind in a small bowl with 3 tablespoons of hot water. Break up the tamarind with a small spoon, then leave it to soak for 20 to 30 minutes. Sieve the mixture to give 3 tablespoons of tamarind liquid and discard any skin and seeds.

Meanwhile, wash the rice in cold water and place it in a large pot. Add 1 litre/1¾ pints of water and a little salt. Bring to the boil and simmer for about 20 minutes or until the rice is just soft.

While the rice is cooking, cut the aubergines into 2.5cm/1 in cubes and soak them in a bowl of cold, salted water for 10 minutes. Drain and pat dry with kitchen paper.

Drain the excess water from the cooked rice and set aside.

Heat 1 tablespoon of the oil in a small saucepan, then add the mustard seeds, black gram dal, curry leaves, dried red chillies and cinnamon and cook until the dal is brown. Add the coconut and cook, stirring constantly, for a few minutes until golden brown. Remove from the heat and leave to cool slightly. Transfer the mixture to a blender, add the tamarind liquid and grind to a paste.

Heat the remaining oil in a large frying pan, add the onion and cook until brown. Add the lime juice, turmeric and chilli powder and stir until the mixture is well blended.

Add the aubergine to the frying pan and cook for 10 minutes, stirring frequently. Stir the spicy coconut paste into the aubergine sauce and season to taste. When the aubergine is tender, mix in the cooked rice and half the chopped coriander. Transfer to a serving dish, garnish with the remaining coriander and serve hot.

Peas pilau rice

To most people in Kerala, this rice dish is for special occasions. Normally they eat plain boiled rice with all their dishes. Ghee, milk and saffron are too expensive to use in everyday cooking, so this way of serving rice makes a meal festive and different. In the UK, however, it is a different matter – this is the most common rice dish in Indian-style restaurants. It's very easy to prepare and can be served with any vegetable curry, whether mild or hot. Alternatively, it can be served with plain raita.

serves 4

250g/9 oz basmati rice

5 tablespoons milk

5 saffron threads

8 tablespoons vegetable oil

1 large onion, finely chopped

25g/1 oz raw cashew nuts

5 cardamom pods

5 cloves

5 black peppercorns

2 bay leaves

1 cinnamon stick

125g/4½ oz green peas

1 tablespoon ghee (optional)

salt

Wash the rice thoroughly and set aside to drain. Heat the milk in a small saucepan to just below scalding point and add the saffron. Stir, then remove from the heat and set aside to infuse.

Heat 3 tablespoons of the oil in a small frying pan and add half the onion. Cook over a medium heat until the onion is well browned and crisp. Remove and set aside to drain on kitchen paper until ready to serve.

In a large saucepan, heat the remaining oil and add the cashew nuts, cardamom, cloves, peppercorns, bay leaves and cinnamon. Cook, stirring, over a medium heat for 2 minutes until the mixture is fragrant.

Add the remaining raw onion to the spices and cook, stirring, until the onion is lightly browned. Stir in the rice and 1 litre/1¾ pints of water. Add a little salt and the peas, then lower the heat right down, cover and cook for about 20 minutes or until the rice is tender but firm. If the rice becomes too dry during cooking, add some more water.

Drain the rice to remove any excess water, then return it to the saucepan and stir in the saffron milk and ghee, if using. Garnish with the reserved crisp onions and serve hot.

Curd rice

You could call this unusual Tamil speciality a salad. Light and clean-tasting, it leaves the palate wonderfully refreshed and is a cooling complement to hotter dishes. Curd rice is generally served at the end of Indian feasts, although the Tamils of Palakkad, the town on the border of Kerala and Tamil Nadu, also eat it at lunchtime. It is best served topped with a piquant pickle such as chilli and ginger pickle *(see page 45).*

serves 4

600g/1 lb 5 oz basmati rice
1 tablespoon vegetable oil
¹/₂ teaspoon mustard seeds
a few curry leaves
1 dried red chilli
1cm/¹/₂ in fresh root ginger, finely chopped
1.2 litres/2 pints plain yogurt
120ml/4 fl oz milk
3 fresh green chillies, finely sliced
salt

Wash the rice in cold water and place it in a large pot. Cover generously with water and add a little salt. Bring to the boil and simmer for about 20 minutes or until the rice is just tender. Drain the excess water from the rice and set aside.

Heat the oil in a small frying pan and add the mustard seeds. As they begin to pop, add the curry leaves, dried red chilli and ginger. When the ginger turns golden brown, pour the contents of the pan over the rice and mix thoroughly.

In a mixing bowl, whisk the yogurt with a pinch of salt. Gradually add the yogurt to the rice, stirring slowly and continuously. Stir in the milk and mix thoroughly. Serve topped with the green chillies and some pickles.

curries

curries

Curry is the word most often associated with Indian food, but your understanding of the term may be very different to mine. As a child in Kerala I was taught that curry means the sauce or gravy of a dish, and if one wanted more sauce with a meal one would ask for curry. However, curry is the word that seems to define all Indian food around the world today. Britain has around 10,000 so-called Indian restaurants serving 'curries' and many supermarkets claim curries are the best-selling ready-meals on their shelves. For the purposes of clarity: this chapter contains saucy dishes.

As I hope you can see from the rest of this book, my home state of Kerala offers some of India's most diverse dishes. Our meals vary in colour, flavour, aroma and texture and we tend to enjoy change and variety in our food more than the people of North India. Keralan curries are simple and light most of the time, refreshingly spiced and traditionally eaten with rice. I have been most inspired by the simple approach of Kerala's Brahmins (upper class Hindus), who use many different vegetables and pulses in their cooking.

Here I aim to use the best of my experience to bring you a comprehensive selection of the most outstanding vegetable and fruit curries available to both vegetarians and meat eaters. Carnivores often comment that they never miss meat when eating at Rasa, even though they love meat. That is very encouraging and satisfying to me, and motivation to continue creating and cooking vegetarian curry dishes for everybody who loves this kind of food.

Avial

A mixture of vegetables cooked in a light blend of spices, coconut and tangy yogurt, avial is the traditional festival dish of Kerala and no wedding or feast would be complete without it. Even meat eaters think it is essential. The array of colours makes it perfect celebration food. It is perhaps South India's best-known vegetable curry and often on the menus of British Indian restaurants that otherwise serve North Indian food. In your home, serve avial with basmati rice and cucumber raita.

serves 4

100g/3½ oz drumsticks
100g/3½ oz carrots
200g/7 oz potatoes
2.5cm/1 in cube root ginger, peeled and chopped
1 fresh green chilli, chopped
1 teaspoon cumin seeds
100g/3½ oz green beans
100g/3½ oz green mango (optional)
1 teaspoon turmeric powder
1 teaspoon salt, or more to taste
200g/7 oz plain yogurt
3 tablespoons freshly grated coconut,
  or 5 tablespoons desiccated coconut
about 20 curry leaves

Cut all the vegetables into 5cm/2 in fingers about 1cm/½ in thick. Place the drumsticks and carrots in a large heavy saucepan and cover with water. Bring to the boil and cook for 5 minutes, stirring occasionally. Add the potatoes and leave to cook over a medium heat, stirring occasionally, for 10 to 15 minutes until the potatoes are not quite tender.

Meanwhile, place the ginger, chilli and cumin in a pestle and mortar with 1 tablespoon of water and crush to a smooth paste. Alternatively, use a grinder.

When the potatoes and carrots are nearly cooked, stir in the green beans, mango (if using), turmeric, salt and ginger paste. Lower the heat, cover and simmer for 5 minutes, stirring occasionally, until all the vegetables are cooked.

Add the yogurt and coconut, mix well, then add the curry leaves. Heat the mixture through gently before serving but do not let it boil.

Kayi korma curry

Chef Narayanan loves innovation and I was lucky to learn from his talent and when we were compiling new menus for the various Rasa restaurants. This dish is something he came up with when I wanted him to suggest a curry to complement idiappam and appam bread. According to him, it can be made from any vegetable you choose and certainly in India we tend to make mixed vegetable curries according to what's left in the pantry from the day before. Although there are hundreds of recipes for such dishes, this one is particularly easy and attractive. Cashews and coconut give richness to balance the lightness of idiappam and appams.

serves 4

50g/1³/₄ oz freshly grated or desiccated coconut

50g/1³/₄ oz cashew nuts

6 tablespoons vegetable oil

1 teaspoon mustard seeds

1 onion, finely chopped

5 fresh green chillies, finely chopped

10 curry leaves

2.5cm/1 in root ginger, finely chopped

1 teaspoon turmeric powder

1 teaspoon chilli powder

1 teaspoon tomato paste

1 green bell pepper, cubed

1 red bell pepper, cubed

100g/3¹/₂ oz carrots, cubed

100g/3¹/₂ oz potatoes, cubed

50g/1³/₄ oz green peas

In a blender or food processor, grind the coconut, cashews and 570ml/1 pint of water to a fine paste.

Heat the oil in a large pan and add the mustard seeds. As they begin to pop, add the onion, green chillies, curry leaves and ginger. Sauté for 10 minutes until the onion is brown.

Add the turmeric, chilli powder and tomato paste. Blend well and cook over a low heat for 5 minutes.

Stir in the coconut paste and 1.2 litres/2 pints of water. Bring the mixture to the boil, then add the cubed vegetables and peas and cook for 10 minutes or until the vegetables are tender.

Lower the heat, cover the pan and cook for a further 5 minutes. Serve hot with iddiappam, appam, paratha or chapatti *(see pages 49–55)*.

Broccoli and coconut curry

It was a pleasant revelation to have a Spanish broccoli dish at a friend's house. That occasion was probably the first time I really ate broccoli – March 1993, just after my wedding to Alison. The vegetable has fascinated me ever since and I have tried many different ways of combining it with Keralan spices. The general manager of Rasa restaurants, Preeta Nair, has inspired me to experiment with new vegetables and create our own specialities for Rasa. She was right: I now find it more satisfying to devise new dishes and make Indian food more interesting to new converts and people who love change. Cook broccoli carefully so that the colour and texture is bright and healthy.

serves 4

1 teaspoon ghee or butter
6 shallots, cut into wedges
1 1/2 teaspoons plain flour
3 tablespoons tomato paste
1/2 teaspoon chilli powder
1/2 teaspoon ground coriander
1/2 teaspoon turmeric powder
350g/12 oz broccoli, cut into florets
150g/5 oz potato, cut into batons
250ml/9 fl oz coconut milk

In a large saucepan, heat the ghee or butter. Add the shallots and fry for 5 minutes or until brown. Remove the pan from the heat and sprinkle the flour over the shallots. Mix well and return the pan to a low heat.

Slowly add 450ml/16 fl oz of water, stirring constantly to avoid lumps. Mix in the tomato paste, chilli, coriander and turmeric and cook for 2 minutes.

Add the broccoli and potato and simmer, stirring occasionally, for 20 minutes or until the vegetables are tender.

Lower the heat right down and add the coconut milk. Cook, stirring constantly, for a further 5 minutes then serve immediately.

Cucumber curry

This is a simplified version of a traditional white pumpkin dish my mum used to make in summertime, although pumpkin dishes are very popular throughout the year in Kerala. Many varieties are available in my village. Their tastes – as well as their colours and shapes – are all very different. Although I'm suggesting that you make this particular dish with cucumbers, try it one day with the authentic white pumpkins, which take a bit longer to cook.

serves 4

1 tablespoon tamarind pulp
¹/₂ teaspoon fenugreek seeds
4 dried red chillies
50g/2 oz freshly grated or desiccated coconut
1 teaspoon turmeric powder
4 tablespoons vegetable oil
¹/₂ teaspoon mustard seeds
7 curry leaves
400g/14 oz cucumber, finely chopped

Steep the tamarind in 4 tablespoons of hot water, breaking up the pulp as much as possible with a small spoon. Leave to soak for 20 to 30 minutes, then sieve the mixture to give 4 tablespoons of tamarind liquid.

Meanwhile, in a frying pan, dry-toast the fenugreek and chillies for 1 minute over a low heat.

Place the toasted fenugreek and chillies, coconut, turmeric and tamarind juice in a blender or grinder and grind to a fine paste.

Heat the oil in the frying pan. Add the mustard seeds and, as they begin to pop, add the curry leaves and the ground coconut mixture. Cook, stirring, until the mixture is relatively hot, then add the cucumber and cook for 5 minutes over a low heat, mixing well. Serve hot.

Carrot pachadi

In Kerala, dishes with thick yogurt sauces or pachadis are very popular for weddings. We make many different pachadis with various fruits and vegetables – beetroot and pineapple are very popular for special occasions. Carrot pachadi is something I discovered when I came to Britain and went to a wedding feast at the Murughan Temple in East Ham, London. It was created by a famous temple chef, Ram Narayan. It was delicious, with a beautiful vibrant colour and much more refreshing than beetroot pachadi. Best of all, carrots are cheap and plentiful. This dish goes well with rice or bread.

serves 4

100g/3 1/2 oz freshly grated coconut
2 fresh green chillies, chopped
5mm/1/4 in cube root ginger, peeled
1 teaspoon ground mustard seeds
2 tablespoons vegetable oil
2 teaspoons mustard seeds
10 curry leaves
4 large carrots, shredded
1 teaspoon chilli powder
1 teaspoon turmeric powder
225ml/8 fl oz plain yogurt
salt

In a spice mill, finely grind the coconut, fresh chillies, ginger and ground mustard together. Set aside.

Heat the oil in a large frying pan or wok. Add the whole mustard seeds and, as they begin to pop, add the curry leaves. Stir in the shredded carrots, chilli powder, turmeric and a little salt and cook for 10 minutes over a medium heat, stirring frequently.

Stir in the ground coconut mixture. Lower the heat, cover and cook for 10 minutes, stirring often. Remove from the heat and stir in the yogurt. Serve hot or cold.

Carrot and onion sambar

Sambar is one of the most popular curries in South India, and one of the most versatile. They can be made with a wide variety of ingredients but the basic spicing stays the same. Sambar is most commonly served with dosas or vadai. At breakfast they are the essential accompaniment to idlies. At an elaborate meal or feast, sambar is the first dish that goes on top of the banana leaf, so people say, 'If you know how to make a good sambar, you can cook South Indian food.' However, these days, I'm inclined to think North Indians like sambar more than their Southern counterparts.

serves 4

1 tablespoon tamarind pulp

150g/5 oz toor dal

3 fresh green chillies, slit lengthways

1 teaspoon turmeric powder

1 teaspoon chilli powder

4 onions, cut into 2.5cm/1 in cubes

4 carrots, sliced

2 tomatoes, quartered

100g/3½ oz freshly grated or desiccated coconut

2 teaspoons coriander seeds

1 tablespoon lemon juice

2 tablespoons vegetable oil

2 teaspoons mustard seeds

1 teaspoon fenugreek

10 curry leaves

4 dried red chillies

salt

Combine the tamarind pulp with 4 tablespoons of hot water in a small bowl. Leave to soak for 20 to 30 minutes, stirring occasionally to help dissolve the tamarind. Sieve the mixture to give 4 tablespoons of tamarind liquid.

Bring 300ml/11 fl oz of water to the boil in a large saucepan. Add the toor dal, fresh green chillies, turmeric and chilli powder. Simmer for 15 minutes or until the lentils are well cooked.

Add the onions, carrots, tomatoes, tamarind liquid and salt to taste. Cover and cook for 5 minutes.

Meanwhile, place the coconut, coriander and 50ml/2 fl oz of water in a grinder and grind to a fine paste. Add to the vegetables in the pan, cover again and cook for a further 10 minutes.

Add the lemon juice to the pan, stir thoroughly and remove from the heat.

Heat the oil in a small frying pan. Add the mustard seeds and, as they begin to pop, add the fenugreek, curry leaves and dried red chillies. Pour the contents of the pan over the curry and gently stir through. Serve hot.

Ulli theeyal

Not for the faint-hearted, this strongly flavoured shallot curry complements any meal but is particularly good served with dosas to add extra texture and taste. It comes from the Nair community, which plays an important role in the history of Keralan cooking and of which I am a proud member. They are the originators of many of South India's most famous speciality dishes and a meal with a Nair family is widely considered to be the best vegetarian meal you can have. To make this curry more substantial, you could add vegetables like plantains, drumsticks and potatoes, but I love using shallots alone because the masala sauce perfectly matches the sweetness of the shallots.

serves 4

1 teaspoon tamarind pulp

5 tablespoons vegetable oil

250g/9 oz shallots, peeled and halved

2 fresh green chillies, slit lengthways

1 teaspoon turmeric powder

3 tomatoes, quartered

1 teaspoon mustard seeds

10 curry leaves

salt

for the masala paste:

50g/2 oz freshly grated or desiccated coconut

2 tablespoons coriander seeds

3 dried red chillies

10 curry leaves

1 clove garlic

a small piece of cinnamon stick

Place the tamarind pulp in a small bowl with 4 teaspoons of hot water. Leave to soften for 20 to 30 minutes, stirring occasionally to help the tamarind dissolve. Sieve the mixture to give 4 teaspoons of tamarind liquid.

Meanwhile, in a large frying pan, dry-toast all the ingredients for the masala until the coconut turns brown. Remove from the heat and leave to cool for 5 minutes. Transfer to a blender, add 450ml/16 fl oz of water and grind well to form a liquid paste.

In a kadai, wok or large saucepan, heat 4 tablespoons of the oil. Add the shallots and chillies and cook for 5 minutes or until the shallots are soft. Add the turmeric powder, some salt and the ground masala. Cook over a medium heat for 5 minutes.

Mix in the tomatoes and tamarind liquid and continue cooking until the onions are very tender.

Heat the remaining oil in a frying pan. Add the mustard seeds and, as they begin to pop, add the curry leaves. Pour the contents of the pan over the curry, stir through, and cook over a medium heat for 3 minutes before serving.

Veluthulli curry

London Mayor Ken Livingstone wrote about Rasa W1 in the *Evening Standard* magazine, recommending that people visit the restaurant just to try their first curry made solely from garlic. Are you too scared? People who love garlic think this is a treat. I have never needed any special incentive to eat garlic, having loved it since I was a little boy. It is, indeed, pungent, but that is part of the attraction and in India every-one believes it cleanses the blood. Garlic may be an acquired taste but once you fall under its spell there is no getting away. When making this dish, be sure to cook the garlic very well to enjoy it at its best.

serves 4

75g/3 oz tamarind pulp
6 tablespoons vegetable oil
1/2 teaspoon fennel seeds
1/2 teaspoon fenugreek seeds
10 curry leaves
3 onions, finely chopped
2 fresh green chillies, finely chopped
1/2 teaspoon turmeric powder
1/2 teaspoon chilli powder
2 tomatoes, finely chopped
200g/7 oz garlic cloves, peeled

Place the tamarind pulp in a small bowl with 850ml/1 1/2 pints of hot water. Break up the tamarind pulp as much as possible and leave to soak for 20 to 30 minutes. Sieve the mixture to give a bowl of tamarind liquid. Discard the skin and seeds.

In a large pan, heat the oil and add the fennel and fenugreek. Briefly sauté until the spices turn brown, then add the curry leaves, onions and green chillies. Cook over a medium heat for 5 minutes until the onions are soft.

Add the turmeric and chilli powder, mix well, then add the tomatoes. Cook for 5 minutes to give a thick onion gravy.

Mix in the garlic, then the tamarind liquid. Lower the heat and cook for 15 minutes or until the mixture is thick and the garlic is well cooked. Serve with paratha *(see pages 49–50)*.

tamarind pod

Mixed pepper curry

Maybe it is because bell peppers are an unusual vegetable in Kerala that I always seem to fancy a bell pepper dish with my meals. Or maybe it's because I love the taste of chillies and bell peppers have a light chilli flavour. When I came to Britain I was amazed by the colours of all the peppers in the stores and was enthusiastic about using them at Rasa. We started with refreshing chutneys and stir-fried dishes, but developing a bell pepper curry was a challenge. This one is sweet and simple and adds a wonderful colour to any Keralan meal. It goes very well with paratha and can be served as a light lunch.

serves 4

3 tablespoons vegetable oil

1 teaspoon mustard seeds

1 teaspoon turmeric powder

1 teaspoon chilli powder, or more to taste

1 teaspoon cumin seeds

3–4 curry leaves

500g/1 lb 2 oz mixed bell peppers, seeded and finely sliced

salt

Heat the oil in a large saucepan. Add the mustard seeds and, as they begin to pop, add the turmeric, salt to taste, chilli, cumin and curry leaves. Cook, stirring, for 2 to 3 minutes.

Add the bell peppers and 2 tablespoons of water. Cover and cook for approximately 15 minutes, stirring occasionally, until the peppers are tender. Serve hot.

Cabbage curry

Cabbage is one of the favourite leaf vegetables in South Indian homes, probably because it is easy to cook and available most of the year. Dry stir-fried dishes of crispy greens are very common as part of day-to-day meals as well as at feasts for special occasions. Cabbage in a curry form, however, is quite unusual but this dish is light and simple.

serves 4

1 tablespoon tamarind pulp

25g/1 oz chana dal

500g/1 lb 2 oz cabbage, chopped

100g/3½ oz green peas

1 teaspoon turmeric powder

1 teaspoon chilli powder

2 tomatoes, finely chopped

4 tablespoons vegetable oil

1 teaspoon mustard seeds

5 curry leaves

2 cloves garlic

1 large onion, sliced

1 teaspoon cumin seeds

1 teaspoon coriander seeds

25g/1 oz freshly grated or desiccated coconut

salt

In a small bowl, steep the tamarind pulp in 4 tablespoons of hot water. Leave the mixture to soak for 20 to 30 minutes, stirring periodically to help break down the tamarind. Sieve the mixture to give 4 tablespoons of tamarind liquid.

Meanwhile, in a small saucepan, cook the chana dal in a generous quantity of boiling water for 15 minutes, then drain and set aside.

In another saucepan, bring 450ml/16 fl oz of water to the boil. Add the cabbage, peas, turmeric, salt to taste and chilli and cook until the vegetables are tender. Stir in the tomatoes.

Heat the oil in a small frying pan. Add the mustard seeds and, as they begin to pop, add the curry leaves, garlic, onion, cumin and coriander. Sauté for 2 or 3 minutes, then pour the contents of the pan over the cabbage mixture. Pour in the tamarind liquid and mix well.

Add the drained, cooked chana and coconut to the cabbage mixture. Stir to combine and serve hot.

Paneer cheera curry

The combination of spinach and paneer (curd cheese) is a classic of Indian restaurant cooking in Britain. My own version is devised for the taste preferences of my friends rather than according to the traditions of Delhi or Punjab, where the cheese is adored. This recipe is much lighter in oil and has more flavour than similar dishes you may have tried before. Serve it with vegetable paratha *(see page 50)* for a well-balanced meal.

serves 4

100ml/3¹/₂ fl oz vegetable oil, plus
   4 tablespoons extra
50g/2 oz paneer cheese, cut into large cubes
250g/9 oz onion, cubed
2 fresh green chillies
2.5cm/1 in root ginger, chopped
5 curry leaves
250g/9 oz spinach, finely chopped
1 teaspoon turmeric powder
1 teaspoon chilli powder
2 tomatoes, finely chopped
1 green bell pepper, cubed
50ml/1³/₄ fl oz single cream
125ml/4 fl oz milk
salt

Heat 100ml/3¹/₂ fl oz of oil in a frying pan. Add the paneer and fry until lightly browned all over. Remove from the heat, drain off the oil and set the paneer aside.

In a saucepan, heat another 4 tablespoons of oil. Add the onion, green chillies, ginger and curry leaves. Cook for 5 minutes, stirring occasionally, until the onions are soft.

Add the spinach, turmeric, chilli powder and some salt, then the tomatoes and green bell pepper. Cook for 5 minutes. Stir in the cream and milk. Bring the mixture to a boil, stirring constantly, then remove the pan from the heat and add the fried paneer. Mix well and serve hot.

Cheera thayir curry

My mother's special recipe: she makes this when the whole family gets together. The combination of spinach and yogurt is a particular favourite with people in Kerala, although we normally use red spinach. When I came to Britain I tried this variation using green English spinach and, to my pleasure, our customers liked it a lot. It is a nice refreshing combination.

serves 4

4 tablespoons vegetable oil
2 teaspoons mustard seeds
3 cloves garlic, finely chopped
3 dried red chillies
10 curry leaves
a pinch of fenugreek
2 onions, finely chopped
3 fresh green chillies, slit lengthways
2.5cm/1 in ginger, finely chopped
2 tomatoes, finely chopped
1 teaspoon turmeric powder
150g/5 oz spinach, trimmed
250g/9 oz plain yogurt
salt

Heat the oil in a large saucepan. Add the mustard seeds and, as they begin to pop, add the garlic, dried red chillies, curry leaves and fenugreek. Cook, stirring frequently, over a medium heat, for 2 minutes, then add the onions, green chillies and ginger.

When the onion turns brown, add the tomatoes, turmeric and some salt. Mix thoroughly, then add the spinach and cook for 5 minutes, stirring occasionally.

Remove the pan from the heat. Gradually add the yogurt, stirring slowly and continuously. Return the pan to the heat for a further 5 minutes, stirring constantly. Serve lukewarm.

Vendekka cheera kozhambu

Many people do not like okra because it can be slimy, which happens when the vegetable is cooked for a long time. I think it is best when slightly crunchy and cooked quickly. In fact, okra is incredibly versatile, simple to use and the texture and colour are inviting, so it's a pleasure to use creatively. This wonderful dish combines it with several other of my favourite ingredients including spinach, coconut milk and yogurt. It can be served either hot or cold, preferably with plain rice as part of a selection of dishes.

serves 4

225g/8 oz plain yogurt
50ml/2 fl oz coconut milk
5 tablespoons vegetable oil
1 teaspoon mustard seeds
2 onions, finely chopped
5 curry leaves
1 teaspoon ground coriander
1 teaspoon turmeric powder
1/2 teaspoon chilli powder
250g/9 oz spinach, trimmed
100g/3 1/2 oz fresh okra, cut into 1cm/1/2 in pieces
salt

Combine the yogurt and coconut milk in a blender. Blend until smooth, then set aside.

Heat the oil in a large saucepan. Add the mustard seeds and, as they begin to pop, add the onions and curry leaves. Sauté until the onion turns brown. Add the coriander, turmeric, chilli and some salt. Mix well and cook for 2 to 3 minutes over a low heat.

Add the spinach and cook for 5 minutes, or until the spinach wilts. Add the okra and cook for a further 5 minutes.

Stir in the yogurt and coconut mixture and cook over a low heat for 2 or 3 minutes, then serve hot.

Cauliflower and potato curry

Cauliflower is a 'foreign' vegetable in Kerala. In winter they are brought from North India to add more variety and flair to our cooking. Usually when South Indians cook a cauliflower, they follow similar methods to those used for the North Indian delicacies. This is a variation, in our style, of the well-known North Indian dish aloo gobi.

serves 4

200g/7 oz potatoes, peeled
200g/7 oz cauliflower
4 tablespoons vegetable oil
1 teaspoon fennel seeds
1 large onion, finely chopped
1/2 teaspoon turmeric powder
1/2 teaspoon chilli powder
4 tablespoons tomato paste
4 tomatoes, quartered
100ml/3 1/2 fl oz milk
a small bunch of fresh coriander,
  finely chopped
salt

Cut the potatoes into large chunks and break the cauliflower into florets.

Heat the oil in a medium saucepan and add the fennel. Cook, stirring, until browned, then add the onion and cook for 10 minutes until the onion is also brown. Add the turmeric and chilli and stir-fry for 2 minutes, then stir in the tomato paste.

Add the potato, cauliflower, tomatoes, milk, some salt and 100ml/3 1/2 fl oz of water. Cook over a medium heat, stirring constantly to prevent the milk splitting. When the potatoes are completely tender, add the coriander, mix well and serve hot.

Pal curry

Fragrant and mild, this milky potato stew is loved by those who are not very keen on spices. It is a favourite of Kerala's Christian community and is always served during Easter, but generally not found in other parts of India. Pal curry is best eaten with appam, but can also be served with plain rice. In 'God's own country', which Kerala is often called, the combination of a pure white potato stew gently spiced with fresh green chillies, simmered in hand-squeezed coconut milk served with spongy sweet white appam pancake is one even God would like to eat, any time of the day.

serves 4

4 tablespoons vegetable oil

1 cinnamon stick

2 cardamom pods

2 cloves

1 bay leaf

2 large onions, finely sliced

1 tomato, quartered

3 green chillies, slit lengthways

4cm/1½ in fresh root ginger, peeled and cut into very fine strips

250g/9 oz potatoes, peeled and cubed

570ml/1 pint milk

400ml/14 fl oz coconut milk

salt

Heat the oil in a large saucepan. Add the cinnamon, cardamom, cloves and bay leaf and cook, stirring, for 2 to 3 minutes or until fragrant.

Add the onion and cook for 5 minutes or until it is soft. Add the tomato, chillies, salt and ginger and cook, stirring, for 2 minutes. Then add the potatoes and milk and cook over a gentle heat for 5 minutes, stirring constantly.

Pour in the coconut milk and 100ml/3½ fl oz of water. Cook gently for 10 minutes until the potatoes are tender, stirring constantly. Serve hot.

Yam in yogurt sauce

Yam, like cassava, is seen all over Kerala as a staple starch. Every house in the state has a back garden full of home-grown vegetables, and yams – like other root vegetables – grow abundantly. The plant has a flourishing umbrella of green leaves with thin stems. Yams need thorough washing to remove the soil stuck to the skin, and then must be carefully peeled to reveal the pinkish interior. We normally cut it into cubes like potato. When cooked for a long time, yam turns soft like sweet potato and melts in your mouth.

serves 4

2 teaspoons turmeric powder

450g/1 lb yam, peeled and cut into chunks

2 tablespoons vegetable oil

1 teaspoon mustard seeds

2 onions, finely sliced

10 curry leaves

3 dried red chillies

2.5cm/1 in fresh ginger, finely sliced

2 fresh green chillies, slit lengthways

400ml/14 fl oz yogurt

salt

Heat a large saucepan of salted water to boiling point. Add 1 teaspoon of the turmeric, then the yam. Cover and cook over a medium heat for 15 minutes or until the yam is tender. Drain and set aside.

Wipe out the pan and return to the heat with the oil. Add the mustard seeds and, as they begin to pop, add the onions, curry leaves, dried red chillies, ginger and some salt. Cook, stirring frequently, over a medium heat for 5 minutes or until the onion has browned.

Add the cooked yam and fresh green chillies to the onion mixture, stir thoroughly and cook for 1 minute. Add the remaining turmeric, mix well, then remove the pan from the heat.

Gradually add the yogurt, mixing slowly and continuously. Return the pan to the heat for 1 minute, still stirring constantly, then serve lukewarm.

Kadala curry

Chickpeas are very popular all over India. In Kerala we have a habit of eating them in the morning with breakfast dishes such as appams and steamed rice pancakes called puttu. Our use of coconut makes the chickpeas taste very different from the famous North Indian dish chana masala. Using canned chickpeas and coconut milk saves a lot of time – dried chickpeas can take up to 3 hours to cook thoroughly, not including the soaking time.

serves 4

1 tablespoon tamarind pulp
3 medium onions
3 tomatoes
6 tablespoons vegetable oil
2.5cm/1 in cinnamon stick
1 teaspoon turmeric powder
1 teaspoon chilli powder
400g/14 oz can chickpeas
200ml/7 fl oz coconut milk
1 teaspoon mustard seeds
10 curry leaves
4 dried red chillies

for the masala:

100g/3½ oz freshly grated or desiccated coconut
2 tablespoons coriander seeds
8 curry leaves
2 cloves garlic, finely sliced
3 dried red chillies

In a small bowl, place the tamarind pulp and cover with 3 tablespoons of water. Leave the tamarind to dissolve, then strain to give 3 tablespoons of tamarind liquid. Meanwhile, cut the onions into 2.5cm/1 in cubes, quarter the tomatoes, and set aside separately.

To make the masala, toast all the ingredients in a dry frying pan over a low heat for about 5 minutes or until the coconut and coriander seeds turn brown. Cool slightly, then transfer the mixture to a blender. Add 450ml/16 fl oz of water and grind to a fine, liquid paste. Set aside.

In a large saucepan, heat 3 tablespoons of the oil. Add the cinnamon stick and onions and cook for 5 minutes or until the onions are soft and transparent. Add the turmeric and chilli powder, mix well, then add the chickpeas and tomatoes.

Add the masala paste to the onion mixture and cook over a low heat for 10 minutes. Stir in the coconut milk and tamarind liquid. Turn the heat right down and stir thoroughly.

In a small frying pan, heat the remaining oil. Add the mustard seeds and, as they begin to pop, add the curry leaves and dried red chillies. Pour the mixture into the chickpea curry, stir well and remove from the heat. Serve with bread, pancakes or idiappam *(see page 53)*.

Drumstick parippu curry

Raghu, my friend who works in Rasa W1, loves drumsticks more than any other vegetable and frequently asks me to make dishes from them. I always manage to come up with something for him because it is nice to cook for people who love food. Parippu curry is the only dish Raghu can make himself, so it was a strange coincidence when I devised this dish for him. Drumsticks are one of Kerala's most unusual vegetables. Sadly, there are no appropriate substitutes to use instead but drumsticks can be obtained in Britain from Indian grocery shops. They are very long and have a fibrous outer husk that does not soften when cooked. Use your hands to help you eat the soft flesh inside the drumstick – and be prepared to get a bit messy (that is the best part).

serves 4

25g/1 oz tamarind pulp
250g/9 oz mung beans
4 drumsticks, cut into 5cm/2 in pieces
3 fresh green chillies, finely sliced
2 cloves garlic, finely sliced
½ teaspoon turmeric powder
½ teaspoon chilli powder
a small bunch of coriander, finely chopped
freshly grated coconut, to garnish
salt

Place the tamarind pulp in a small saucepan and cover with 225ml/8 fl oz of boiling water. Break up as much as possible with a spoon, then cover and leave to steep for 20 to 30 minutes. Sieve the mixture into a clean bowl and discard the seeds and skin. Set aside.

Wash the mung beans to remove any stones, then place them with the drumsticks in a large saucepan with 700ml/24 fl oz of water. Add the fresh green chillies, garlic, turmeric and chilli powder. Place over a high heat and bring to the boil. Lower the heat, then cover and simmer for 30 minutes, stirring occasionally, until the mung beans are soft.

Add the tamarind liquid and salt to taste. Finally, stir in the coriander and serve hot, sprinkled with the coconut.

Mung bean curry

This dish is often made for wedding feasts, yet it is very easy to cook and can be served simply with plain rice. Feel free to replace the mung beans with black eye beans or any other type of dried bean. Mung beans are called cherupayaru in the Malayalam language and occasionally we make a curry that combines them with plantain and yam. However, mung bean and tamarind curry is a combination I learned from a Tamil friend, Mrs Ratnagopal, while celebrating the Pongal festival (the Tamil New Year) in a house in London.

serves 4

25g/1 oz tamarind pulp
250g/9 oz mung beans
3 fresh green chillies, finely sliced
2 cloves garlic, finely sliced
½ teaspoon turmeric powder
½ teaspoon chilli powder
a small bunch of fresh coriander, finely chopped
salt

Place the tamarind pulp in a small saucepan and cover with 225ml/8 fl oz of boiling water. Cover with a lid and leave to soak for 20 to 30 minutes. Sieve the mixture into a clean bowl, discarding the tamarind seeds and skin. Set the tamarind liquid aside.

Meanwhile, wash the mung beans, picking out any stones, then place the beans in a large saucepan with 725ml/1¼ pints of fresh water. Add the green chillies, garlic, turmeric and chilli powder and place over a high heat. Bring to the boil, then lower the heat, cover and simmer for 30 minutes, stirring occasionally.

When the mung beans are soft, add the tamarind liquid and salt to taste. Stir in the coriander and serve hot.

Pancha phalam

The first time I had this fruit curry was at a Namboothiri (upper caste Hindu) household in our village, almost 25 years ago. The function was a wedding and they made a lot of unusual dishes that we Nairs were not used to. Pancha phalam really fascinated me because, other than mango, we hardly used fruits in our cooking. Years later, I met the chef who prepared lunch that day and he taught me how to make it. To my surprise, it was very easy.

serves 4

200g/7 oz pineapple

1 ripe plantain, peeled

100g/3¹/₂ oz seedless white grapes

100g/3¹/₂ oz seedless red grapes

50g/2 oz jaggery

1 teaspoon turmeric powder

2 tablespoons vegetable oil

1 teaspoon mustard seeds

10 curry leaves

3 dried red chillies

salt

for the masala:

100g/3¹/₂ oz freshly grated or desiccated coconut

4 fresh green chillies

1 tablespoon mustard powder

Cut the pineapple and plantain into 2.5cm/1 in cubes and halve the grapes if you prefer.

Grind the ingredients for the masala in a blender to give a coarse paste.

Place the pineapple in a large saucepan and cover generously with water. Bring to the boil and simmer for 5 minutes. Add the plantain, jaggery, turmeric and salt and continue simmering for another 5 minutes until the fruit is thoroughly cooked and the jaggery well blended.

Stir in the masala paste, lower the heat and cook gently for 5 minutes. Gently mix in the grapes.

In a separate pan, heat the oil. Add the mustard seeds and, as they begin to pop, add the curry leaves and red chillies and cook for 1 minute. Pour the oil mixture over the curry, stir and serve hot.

Nellika curry

Not a well-known curry, this very unusual gooseberry dish is normally eaten in tiny quantities due to its sourness. It has to be eaten with other dishes as part of a large meal. Gooseberries have a wonderful cleansing and refreshing quality in the mouth, making you more sensitive to the other flavours in an Indian feast.

serves 4

1 teaspoon tamarind pulp

3 tablespoons vegetable oil

1 teaspoon mustard seeds

4 shallots, finely sliced

10 curry leaves

250g/9 oz gooseberries, picked over

4 fresh green chillies, slit lengthways

1/2 teaspoon sugar

a pinch of fenugreek seeds

a pinch of asafoetida

salt

for the masala:

50g/2 oz freshly grated or desiccated coconut

2 cloves garlic, chopped

3 teaspoons chilli powder

1 teaspoon turmeric powder

1 teaspoon mustard seeds

Place the tamarind in a small bowl and cover with 1 tablespoon of boiling water. Break up the tamarind as much as possible with a spoon, then set aside to steep for 20 minutes. Sieve the mixture to give 1 tablespoon of tamarind liquid and set aside.

Meanwhile, make the masala. In a blender, place the coconut, garlic, chilli powder, turmeric and mustard seeds with 225ml/8 fl oz of water. Grind until fine, then set aside.

Heat the oil in a large frying pan. Add the mustard seeds and, as they begin to pop, add the shallots and curry leaves and cook for 5 minutes over a medium heat until the shallots are soft. Add the gooseberries and fresh green chillies and cook, stirring occasionally, until the berries are soft.

Add the sugar, fenugreek and asafoetida and mix well. When the mixture is thick, add 600ml/21 fl oz of water, lower the heat and cook for 2 minutes.

Stir the ground masala and tamarind liquid into the gooseberry mixture and season to taste with salt. Increase the heat and bring the mixture to the boil. Simmer for 10 minutes until the sauce thickens.

Cover the pan, lower the heat and cook for a further 5 to 10 minutes or until the gooseberries are thoroughly cooked. Serve hot.

soups, side dishes,
thorans and salads

soups

Soups are not something Indians usually think of when it comes to menu planning, as they simply have not been part of our food tradition. The exceptions are the communities with foreign influences such as Christianity, Islam and Judaism. In Kerala, Christians in particular have always enjoyed soups.

India's most famous cookery writers, Mrs K M Mathews and Mrs Thankam Philips, have written a number of innovative, imaginative cookbooks that have helped to create a new Keralan food culture. Their books always feature a good selection of soups and today it has become common to serve soup as a first course in restaurants, even in small towns.

When I opened my first restaurant in London I quickly realised the need to have soups on the menu, so I started trying to create them in my own style of cooking. In addition to traditional rasam, an essence of lentils, tamarind, tomato and spices, we introduced various soups made from vegetables and lentils. Rasam, however, has proved the most popular. This may be thanks to its abundance of delicious spices, but I suspect it is also because Britain has the ideal weather for soup consumption! When made with plenty of black pepper, rasam is an excellent remedy for colds, flu and sore throats. We have many customers who come to our restaurants when they are ill and just ask for this soup. On a cold day, it is the perfect light meal when served with nice bread.

For this chapter I have come up with some new soups to add to the collection offered at Rasa. I hope you like them as much as we do.

Spiced vegetable soup

A wonderful variation of a traditional winter warmer, this simple vegetable mixture has flavourings of chilli, cinnamon and cloves to make a comforting soup ideal for the coldest weather. This recipe was developed in response to a request from a customer for a mixed vegetable soup.

serves 4

100g/3¹/₂ oz spinach, finely chopped
100g/3¹/₂ oz Savoy cabbage
1 fresh green chilli, slit lengthways
1 potato, peeled and chopped
50g/1³/₄ oz carrots, diced
1 tablespoon oil
1 large onion, finely sliced
1 tablespoon ghee or butter
1 cinnamon stick
3 cloves
1 tablespoon plain flour
2 tomatoes, quartered
¹/₂ red bell pepper, finely chopped
salt

In a large saucepan, place the spinach, cabbage and chilli. Cover and cook over a medium heat for 5 minutes or until the spinach is wilted but only half cooked. Remove from the heat and drain. Rinse out the pan for use later.

In another saucepan, bring some salted water to the boil. Add the potato and carrots and simmer for 10 minutes or until tender. Drain and mash roughly.

Heat the oil in a frying pan and add half the sliced onion. Cook for 7 to 10 minutes, stirring occasionally, until the onion is crisp and brown. Remove from the pan and set aside to use as a garnish.

In the cleaned saucepan, heat the ghee or butter. Add the remaining onion, plus the cinnamon and cloves and sauté for 5 minutes or until the onion is soft.

Add the flour and the mashed potato and carrots. Mix well and cook for 2 to 3 minutes.

Add the tomatoes and the wilted green vegetables to the saucepan. Pour in 900ml/30 fl oz of water. Bring to the boil and simmer for 5 minutes over a medium heat, stirring constantly.

Pour the soup into serving bowls. Garnish with the red pepper and crisp onions and serve hot.

Parippu soup

Wherever you go in India, lentil dishes are unavoidable and, for a vegetarian, lentils are one of the key foods for healthy living. We grow various kinds of lentils and pulses in India and make a number of sweets and snacks from them, as well as curries, but producing a soup from lentils was something I had not considered until I came to Britain. At Rasa we have tried making dal soups with many different lentils; this is the one I think is best and we now serve it in all our restaurants.

serves 4

100g/3½ oz toor dal

100g/3½ oz mysore dal

1 onion, finely sliced

1 tomato, diced

4 cloves garlic, finely chopped

2 fresh green chillies, finely sliced

2.5cm/1 in piece fresh root ginger, finely chopped

1 teaspoon chilli powder

1 teaspoon turmeric powder

**4 tablespoons fresh coriander leaves,
   finely chopped**

salt

In a saucepan, combine both dals, the onion, tomato, garlic, chillies, ginger, chilli powder, turmeric and salt. Stir in 1.2 litres/2 pints of water and bring to the boil. Simmer for 20 minutes, stirring often, until the lentils are thoroughly cooked. Sprinkle the coriander over the top of the soup and serve hot.

Garlic and tomato soup

My wife Alison is more fond of soups than me – she could live on them. During one Christmas vacation when I had the opportunity to cook her favourite dishes every day, she agreed one meal to compromise and eat something I would like too. Tomato soup is the dish she asked for that day, and I added garlic because she likes it with everything she eats. As an experiment, it produced very good results which I now pass on to you. Remember to thoroughly wash the dal before starting this recipe.

serves 4

4 tablespoons red dal

1 tablespoon oil

1 teaspoon mustard seeds

10 curry leaves

1 dried red chilli, halved

$\frac{1}{2}$ teaspoon asafoetida

4 large tomatoes, peeled and finely chopped

4 cloves garlic, peeled and halved

2 fresh green chillies

a small piece of fresh root ginger, peeled and finely chopped

$\frac{1}{2}$ teaspoon turmeric powder

a few sprigs of fresh coriander, chopped

salt

Place the washed dal in a large saucepan and add 225ml/8 fl oz of water. Bring to the boil, cover and simmer for 20 minutes until cooked. Remove from the heat and set aside. Do not drain the lentils.

Heat the oil in a large saucepan. Add the mustard seeds and, as they begin to pop, add the curry leaves, red chilli and asafoetida powder. Stirring constantly, add the tomatoes, garlic, green chillies, ginger, turmeric and some salt to taste. Cook for 5 minutes over a moderate heat, then pour the mixture into the pan containing the cooked dal.

Stir in approximately 425ml/15 fl oz of water, or enough to give a thin consistency. Bring the soup back to the boil, stirring. Mix in the coriander and serve hot.

Tomato rasam

Rasam is made in many ways in South India, using a variety of flavours such as tomato, pepper, lemon and cumin, and sometimes all of these together. Despite its long list of ingredients, this soup is very simple to make. Literally translated, rasam means 'essence' and it is served as a second main dish in a meal to complement and help digest rich vegetable dishes. In addition, many people drink rasam as medicine too. When strongly blended with crushed black pepper, ginger and garlic, it is a good remedy for sore throats and colds. I take it when I am sick, and it works.

serves 4

100g/3½ oz tamarind pulp

10 tomatoes, chopped

4 cloves garlic

2.5cm/1 in fresh root ginger, peeled and finely sliced

a small bunch of coriander, finely chopped, plus a few leaves extra to garnish

1 fresh green chilli, slit lengthways

1 teaspoon turmeric powder

½ teaspoon ground black pepper

3 tablespoons oil

1 teaspoon mustard seeds

3 dried red chillies

½ teaspoon cumin seeds

½ teaspoon ground coriander

a few curry leaves

a small pinch of asafoetida

salt

Roughly break up the tamarind pulp with your hands and place the pieces in a mixing bowl. Cover with 450ml/16 fl oz of warm water and leave to soak for 10 minutes. Strain the mixture through a fine sieve into a small bowl, pushing the pulp through the sieve with the back of a spoon. Discard the stones and fibres and set the tamarind liquid aside.

Place the tomatoes, garlic and ginger in a blender and process for 1 minute or until smooth and combined.

In a large saucepan, heat the tamarind liquid over a medium heat for 5 minutes. Add the fresh coriander, green chilli, turmeric, pepper and the blended tomato mixture. Bring the soup to the boil and cook for 15 minutes, stirring occasionally, being careful not to let the mixture boil over.

Add salt to taste, then remove the pan from the heat and set aside.

Heat the oil in a frying pan. Add the mustard seeds and, as they begin to pop, add the red chillies, cumin, ground coriander, curry leaves and asafoetida. Fry for 1 minute, then remove from the heat.

Pour the oil and spices over the soup and stir through. Serve hot, garnished with fresh coriander.

vegetable side dishes

I had no concept of 'side dishes' until I came to the United Kingdom. All the Indian restaurants I visited were keen to suggest one or two side dishes to go with a meal of chicken or meat. Thank goodness, at least this way meat eaters were getting some vegetables, but most of these side dishes were made from the same thick spicy onion and tomato sauce. They were varied only by the vegetables, such as mushroom, aubergine or potato, that were added to the sauce in the pan just before serving.

In the majority of high street curry houses, this practice continues today. Despite many of these venues having more than 100 items on their menu, vegetarians are only able to choose from the side dishes which all have more or less the same taste, and perhaps one proper vegetable curry.

When I devised the first menu for Rasa, I was determined to make things different and interesting. Although it is not really the way we eat in Kerala, I put 'side dishes' on the menu like all the other Indian restaurants, but emphasised variety. I made sure our dishes were individual, with distinct flavours, and often used vegetables that are unusual in Britain, such as kovakka (also known as tindori) and snake gourd.

The dishes here come from the Rasa menu, as well as my own experiences and experiments. As side dishes, they will help to make your dinner table complete when cooking an Indian meal, but they can also be excellent quick main dishes when served simply in the North Indian style with breads like chapattis and paratha.

Snake gourd with dal

Even though many British people are not familiar with the snake gourd – a vegetable that looks rather like a snake – this is one of the most popular dishes in Kerala. Snake gourd is extremely easy to cook and becomes very soft in the process, which is why we use gram dal or lentils in this recipe. They add a particularly crunchy texture that is very different from the dishes many people have come to expect from Indian restaurants. In Britain, you can find snake gourd in many Asian vegetable shops.

serves 4

75g/3 oz red gram dal

1 medium snake gourd, about 500g/1 lb 2 oz, finely chopped

¹/₂ teaspoon turmeric powder

salt

for the masala:

2 teaspoons coconut oil

1 small onion, finely sliced

2 tablespoons urad dal

4 dried red chillies

40g/1¹/₂ oz freshly grated or desiccated coconut

4 teaspoons cumin seeds

1 teaspoon uncooked rice

Wash the red gram dal, then place in a large saucepan and cover with 450ml/16 fl oz of water. Bring to the boil, cover, then lower the heat and simmer gently for 30 minutes or until the lentils are well cooked. Set aside.

To make the masala, heat the coconut oil in a large frying pan. Add the onion and sauté for 5 minutes or until golden brown. Add the urad dal and chillies and continue cooking for another 3 minutes, stirring often to prevent burning.

Remove the onion mixture from the heat and leave to cool a little. Transfer to a blender and add the coconut, cumin, uncooked rice and a little water. Blend the ingredients to a fine paste, adding more water if necessary, then set aside.

Finely chop the snake gourd and place it in a large saucepan. Add the turmeric, a little salt, and 450ml/16 fl oz of water. Bring to the boil and simmer for approximately 20 minutes until the snake gourd is tender.

Add the cooked, undrained dal to the snake gourd. Simmer gently, stirring, for 5 minutes. Add the masala and continue cooking for a few more minutes so that the flavours can meld. Serve hot.

Stuffed aubergines

When aubergines are fried until crisply brown they taste fantastic, and I think baby aubergines are better done this way than cooked in a sauce. I've enjoyed stuffed aubergines in the homes of many Christian friends in Kerala and this particular recipe, known as Enna Kathrikka in Tamil, comes from Mrs Balasubramaniam in Chennai. It's the type of dry, spicy dish that goes best with breads like paratha or chapatti. If baby aubergines are unavailable, just use the smallest you can find. The stuffing can be used for other vegetables including red bell peppers, courgettes and tomatoes.

serves 4

500g/1 lb 2 oz baby aubergines

2 tablespoons vegetable oil

1 tablespoon mustard seeds

1 teaspoon cumin seeds

1 teaspoon urad dal

1 fresh green chilli, halved

a few curry leaves

for the stuffing:

60g/2½ oz freshly grated or desiccated coconut

1 tablespoon vegetable oil

1 teaspoon urad dal

1 tablespoon cumin seeds

½ teaspoon asafoetida

6 dried red chillies

salt

To make the stuffing, place all the ingredients in a large frying pan and toast for 2 to 3 minutes, stirring constantly, until the coconut is golden brown. Turn off the heat and allow the mixture to cool slightly. Transfer to a blender, add the toasted coconut and grind together, adding just enough water to make a thick paste. Set aside.

Working from the globe end, cut the aubergines lengthways into quarters, leaving the stem end intact so that the aubergine is still held together. Heat 1 tablespoon of the oil in a large frying pan and cook the aubergines for 5 minutes until browned, turning occasionally. Set aside to cool.

Fill the inside of each aubergine with the stuffing mixture and set aside.

Heat the remaining oil in a large frying pan and add the mustard seeds, cumin, urad dal, green chilli and curry leaves and cook until the mustard seeds begin to pop. Carefully add the stuffed aubergines to the pan, cover and cook over a low heat for about 5 minutes. Turn the aubergines, being careful not to break them, and continue cooking until tender on each side. Serve hot.

Spice-roasted tomatoes

Mum makes this when the children are hungry and want something quick. It looks basic (and it's cheap), but she always makes it beautifully. This particular blend of spices really brings out the subtle sour flavour of the tomatoes. We eat this dish with chapatti, which are now very popular in Kerala for family dinners.

serves 4

3 tablespoons vegetable oil

5 dried red chillies

2 teaspoons coriander seeds

150g/5 oz tomatoes, halved

1 teaspoon turmeric powder

5 curry leaves

salt

Heat 1 tablespoon of the oil in a large frying pan and fry the chillies and coriander until fragrant. Pour the contents of the pan into a grinder, then grind to a fine paste.

In the same pan, heat the remaining oil. Add the tomatoes, turmeric, salt, curry leaves and spice paste. Cook over a moderate heat, stirring until the tomatoes are thoroughly coated with the flavourings. Serve hot.

red chillies

Chena upperi

Yam is a root vegetable new to the West, but to Keralans it is like the potato is to the British. We tend to use the variety of yam that is pink on the inside. This recipe matches it with spices and coconut but yam also tastes fantastic when cooked with yogurt. The interest from Rasa's customers has been very encouraging. Many of them are trying to become vegetarians and are keen to explore the unusual varieties of vegetables from other countries. Yam is readily available in Asian and African shops.

serves 4

500g/1 lb 2 oz yam, peeled and finely diced
2 teaspoons turmeric powder
1 tablespoon chilli powder
1 tablespoon ground coriander
2 tablespoons vegetable oil
1 tablespoon mustard seeds
5 curry leaves
1 tablespoon urad dal
1 dried red chilli
1 small onion, finely chopped
3 tablespoons freshly grated or desiccated coconut
salt

Place the diced yam in a large saucepan and cover with water. Add the turmeric, chilli powder and coriander, plus a little salt, cover and bring to the boil. Simmer for approximately 30 minutes or until the yam is tender. Drain and set aside.

Heat the oil in the pan. Add the mustard seeds and, as they begin to pop, add the curry leaves, urad dal, dried red chilli and some salt. Stir-fry until the urad dal turns golden.

Add the onion and cook for 5 minutes or until the onion is soft. Add the cooked yam, mix well, then add the coconut and stir through. Serve hot.

Potato podimas

Combining a variety of vegetables with potatoes is typical of the new style of home cooking found in India. This is a dry dish not unlike the popular Bombay potatoes, except that the potatoes are mashed and thoroughly blended with the spices. I think it has a better flavour. Served with paratha or chapattis, it makes a refreshing lunch dish.

serves 4

500g/1 lb 2 oz potatoes, peeled and cubed

3 tablespoons vegetable oil

1 onion, finely chopped

2 fresh green chillies, finely chopped

3 tablespoons freshly grated or desiccated coconut

2.5cm/1 in piece fresh root ginger, peeled and finely chopped

1 tablespoon mustard seeds

1 teaspoon cumin seeds

1 teaspoon urad dal

1/2 teaspoon turmeric powder

1 dried red chilli, halved

2 tablespoons chopped fresh coriander

salt

Cook the potatoes in a large pan of boiling salted water until tender. Drain, then mash roughly and set aside. Rinse out the saucepan.

Heat the oil in the pan and, when hot, add the onion and cook for 5 minutes or until golden brown. Add the green chillies, coconut, ginger, mustard seeds, cumin, urad dal, turmeric and red chilli and mix well. Cook for 5 minutes over a low heat, stirring constantly.

Stir in the mashed potatoes and coriander. When the ingredients are thoroughly combined, serve hot.

Spinach with baby potatoes

According to my father, this dish is a fusion of Indian and English cuisine that originated during colonial times. It reminds me of good old sag aloo, which many British people fondly remember from Indian restaurant menus, but the use of baby potatoes greatly improves the flavour. This goes well with Kerala paratha *(see page 49)* or rice.

serves 4

350g new potatoes, peeled
2 teaspoons turmeric powder
2 tablespoons vegetable oil
2.5cm/1 in fresh root ginger, peeled and
  finely chopped
1 fresh green chilli, sliced
150g/5 oz onions, chopped
2 teaspoons chilli powder
100g/3½ oz tomatoes, sliced
250g/9 oz spinach
salt

Place the potatoes in a large saucepan and cover generously with water. Add ½ teaspoon of the turmeric and some salt and bring to the boil. Cook for 15 minutes or until the potatoes are soft. Drain and set aside.

Heat the oil in a large frying pan over a medium heat. Add the ginger and fresh green chilli and cook for 30 seconds, then add the onion and cook, stirring, until the onion turns slightly golden. Add the chilli powder, the remaining turmeric and some salt and cook, stirring, for another minute.

Add the tomatoes and cook for 5 minutes, stirring, until the tomatoes break down completely. Cover the pan and cook for a further 2 minutes, stirring frequently.

Add the spinach and cook uncovered for 5 to 8 minutes, stirring, until the spinach is wilted. Lower the heat, add the drained potatoes and stir thoroughly to combine. Serve hot.

Spinach and beetroot bhaji

I like spinach, but did not really become enthused about beetroot until I left Kerala. For many beetroot lovers, this unique and simple dish is the best way to enjoy that vegetable – stir-fried in a blend of lightly spiced coconut. The result tastes fresh and crunchy and goes well with yogurt and rice, but I love it served with paratha *(see page 49)*.

serves 4

150g/5 oz raw or cooked beetroot, peeled and finely sliced

5 tablespoons vegetable oil

1½ tablespoons mustard seeds

10 curry leaves

2 dried red chillies

1 onion, finely chopped

1 teaspoon turmeric powder

300g/10½ oz spinach, roughly chopped

50g/2 oz freshly grated or desiccated coconut

salt

If using raw beetroot, cook it in a saucepan of boiling water for 20 minutes or until tender, then drain and set aside; if using ready-cooked beetroot, rinse in a colander under cold water and set aside to drain.

Heat the oil in a large frying pan. Add the mustard seeds and, as they begin to pop, add the curry leaves, chillies and onion. Cook, stirring, for 5 minutes until the onion softens.

Stir in the turmeric, season to taste with salt, then cook for 2 minutes. Add the beetroot and spinach and continue cooking for another 10 minutes, stirring occasionally.

Remove the pan from the heat and add the coconut. Mix well, then transfer to a serving dish and serve hot.

Vendekka roast

Okra (also known as ladies' fingers or bhindi) is here flavoured with spices to give a side dish that will enhance a wide variety of other dishes. My brothers and I used to fight to get a share of this dish after our dad had taken his portion. Cooking the okra whole gives the best flavour but I like to make a small slit along the pointed end of the okra before dropping it into the spices. This dish can be served with any bread or flavoured rice.

serves 4

3 tablespoons vegetable oil

5 dried red chillies

2 teaspoons coriander seeds

150g/5 oz fresh okra, slit lengthways

1 teaspoon turmeric powder

5 curry leaves

salt

Heat 1 tablespoon of the oil in a large frying pan and add the chillies and coriander. When fragrant, pour the mixture into a grinder and grind finely to make a paste. Set aside.

Heat the remaining oil in the pan and add the okra, turmeric, salt, curry leaves and spice paste. Cook over a medium heat for 5 minutes until the okra is tender, stirring well to ensure it is coated with masala. Serve hot.

okra (ladies' fingers or bhindi)

thorans

Dishes of fresh, crunchy stir-fried vegetables flavoured with coconut and curry leaves – thorans – are an essential part of Keralan meals. For a time we lived in an extended family home with dozens of people. The meals were always elaborate, with contributions from all the women living in the house. However, my preferred lunch was always a basic rice dish, yogurt, pickles and one nicely made thoran – just that used to make me very happy.

In my mother's kitchen, chopping vegetables for thoran was my favourite job, especially cutting up greens such as cabbage, long beans and drumstick leaves. Mum's speciality was red spinach and banana stem thoran; it was rather famous locally and as a child I loved eating it more than any other thoran. I remember Mum telling my sister that when you want to learn cooking you should start with thorans because they are very easy to prepare, use only a small number of ingredients and take very little time to cook. Indeed, my sister has learned the right way and became one of the best cooks in our family.

It is exciting to watch thorans being prepared for large parties in India. Giant chopping boards are placed on the floor and hundreds of cabbages, okra and snake gourds are cut up very quickly. They are then cooked in huge pots with a number of hand-grated coconuts added to make excellent thorans in a matter of minutes.

The beauty of the thoran is that it can be made of any vegetable, including greens such as spinach and cabbage, and starchy vegetables including plantain and yam. Thorans are cooked with a minimum of oil and less complicated spicing than curry dishes, but most importantly they bring a healthy and colourful element to the meal. Their role is similar to that of a salad.

When I opened Rasa, Londoners were not familiar with thorans and most of our customers didn't realise that India's cuisine featured side dishes that looked beautiful or tasted fresh and healthy. For them it was a big change from the traditional onion bhaji and bombay aloo culture that had prevailed for a long time, and many now rate thorans amongst their favourite Indian dishes. Give these simple recipes a try and I'm sure you will too.

Drumstick thoran

The drumstick, an unusually long green fibrous vegetable, was a great fascination when we first introduced it at Rasa as part of the vegetable curry avial *(see page 69)*. We even started doing a lentil and drumstick curry and drumstick soup. Funnily enough, a lot of customers started coming to the restaurant just for the drumstick dishes. This recipe is a recent experiment, the idea of our chef Prasad. The result is superb, the combination of the drumstick's rough exterior and soft interior flesh with fresh coconut and onions making it an excellent side dish.

serves 4

200g/7 oz drumsticks
5 tablespoons oil
1 1/2 tablespoons mustard seeds
10 curry leaves
2 dried red chillies
1 onion, finely chopped
1 teaspoon turmeric powder
50g/2 oz freshly grated or desiccated coconut
salt

Cut the drumsticks into 2cm/3/4 in pieces and place in a large saucepan. Cover with water, bring to the boil and simmer for 15 minutes until the drumsticks are tender. Drain and set the drumsticks aside.

Heat the oil in a large frying pan. Add the mustard seeds and, as they begin to pop, add the curry leaves, chillies and onion. Stir-fry for 5 minutes until the onion softens.

Stir in the turmeric, season to taste with salt and stir-fry for another 2 minutes. Add the cooked drumsticks and continue cooking for 3 to 4 minutes.

Remove the pan from the heat. Add the coconut to the thoran and mix well. Transfer to a serving dish and serve hot.

Savoy cabbage thoran

Savoy cabbage is an unusual vegetable in Kerala, unlike white or green cabbages which are often used in thorans, particularly at wedding feasts. I thought it would be interesting to combine the fantastic colour and texture of Savoy cabbage with Indian spices, and the result is this dish, which has a unique taste. To make it more like a traditional thoran, you can add some freshly grated coconut if desired, around 50g/2 oz. I love ordinary cabbage cooked thoroughly to a light brown colour, but I take care to cook Savoy cabbage lightly to keep its colour and texture alive.

serves 4

3 tablespoons oil

2 teaspoons mustard seeds

10 curry leaves

3 teaspoons urad dal

2 onions, finely chopped

2.5cm/1 in piece fresh root ginger, finely chopped

1 teaspoon turmeric powder

1 teaspoon chilli powder

250g/9 oz Savoy cabbage, finely shredded

salt

Heat the oil in a large frying pan. Add the mustard seeds and, as they begin to pop, add the curry leaves and urad dal. Stir-fry until the urad dal turns golden.

Add the onions and cook for 5 minutes or until the onions are soft. Mix in the ginger, turmeric and chilli, then add the Savoy cabbage and some salt.

Sprinkle a little water into the pan, stir well, then cover and cook over a low heat for 15 to 20 minutes, stirring occasionally. The dish is ready when the cabbage is tender.

Bhindi thoran

One of Kerala's most famous thorans is this one, typically served at lunch. Bhindi or okra is a very light, crunchy vegetable when it is freshly cooked. This dish combines it with a lightly spiced onion and coconut masala. As with most other thorans, the coconut gives the dish a nice sweet flavour. The result is a stark contrast to the typical vegetable side dishes of Britain's Indian restaurants, all based on the same spicy-sour tomato and onion gravy. You can use frozen okra for this recipe; it will fry well and quickly if you defrost it before cooking.

serves 4

200g/7 oz okra

5 tablespoons oil

1½ tablespoons mustard seeds

10 curry leaves

2 dried red chillies

1 onion, finely chopped

1 teaspoon turmeric powder

50g/2 oz freshly grated or desiccated coconut

salt

Cut the okra into 1cm/½ in pieces and set aside. Heat the oil in a large frying pan and add the mustard seeds. As they begin to pop, add the curry leaves and chillies, then the onion. Cook, stirring, for 5 minutes until the onion softens.

Stir in the turmeric and a little salt and stir-fry for 2 minutes. Add the okra and cook for another 3 to 4 minutes.

Remove the pan from the heat and add the coconut. Mix well, transfer to a serving dish, and serve hot.

Mezhukku varatti

This thoran is quite different from many other dry dishes we make in Kerala because of the lack of other ingredients that we normally use for thorans. I have seen it served alongside kanji (rice soup) with green mango chutney to accompany. I think it is the perfect combination on a cold day. It you can't find plantains in the stores or markets, you can use green banana as a substitute, but be careful: green banana cooks faster than plantain. Add some freshly grated coconut to this dish if you like, around 50g/2 oz.

serves 4

250g/9 oz green plantains, peeled and cubed

1 teaspoon turmeric powder

3 tablespoons vegetable oil

2 teaspoons mustard seeds

10 curry leaves

3 teaspoons urad dal

2 onions, finely chopped

3 fresh green chillies, slit lengthways

salt

Bring a saucepan of water to the boil, then add the plantain, turmeric and some salt. Cook for 10 minutes or until the plantain is soft. Drain and set aside.

Heat the oil in a large frying pan or wok. Add the mustard seeds and, as they begin to pop, add the curry leaves and urad dal. Cook, stirring, until the urad dal turns golden.

Add the onions and continue cooking for 5 minutes or until the onions are soft. Add the chillies and plantain and mix well. Cook, stirring occasionally, over a low heat for 10 minutes, then serve hot.

Papaya thoran

The most underestimated vegetable or fruit in Kerala is papaya. It is the only vegetable that grows every-where and is available at nobody's cost. I have never seen people using it frequently enough, and as a fruit it is often left to spoil on the tree and be devoured by crows. My mum, however, is one person who used to make thorans occasionally from green papaya. Although papaya grows in Kerala during most seasons, it is most delicious in summer. This thoran is cooked slowly on the stove until the onions are partly caramelised with the spices and acquire a sweet, mellow flavour.

serves 4

5 tablespoons oil

1½ tablespoons mustard seeds

10 curry leaves

2 dried red chillies

1 onion, finely chopped

1 teaspoon turmeric powder

200g/7 oz unripe papaya, peeled and coarsely grated

50g/2 oz freshly grated or desiccated coconut

salt

Heat the oil in a large frying pan. Add the mustard seeds and, as they begin to pop, add the curry leaves, chillies and onion. Cook, stirring, for 5 minutes until the onion softens.

Stir in the turmeric, season to taste with salt, then cook for another 2 minutes. Add the papaya and stir-fry for 10 minutes.

Remove the pan from the heat and add the coconut. Mix well, then transfer to a serving dish and serve hot.

salads

Kerala is a tropical paradise that grows a wide variety of vegetables, fruits and spices. In the mango season, we children used to make fresh crunchy green mango salads. I remember going to the back garden of our house, which is rather like a little forest of mango, jackfruit and bread fruit trees, and having the most fantastic times eating fruits flavoured with shallots, chillies and coconut. Mostly it was during the holidays when we had cousins and friends visiting from other parts of India. They used to love the spicy salads because there was no other way they could enjoy these natural delights at source.

Salad is an essential part of lunch these days in Kerala, although we never had a habit of eating raw vegetables in our traditional meals. Now people are more aware of the need to eat healthily and including salad with a meal makes it fresh and colourful. Indians often eat street food for lunch, which has also helped make salads more popular. People from small villages go to the cities with their fruit baskets, little bowls made of leaves, and lots of masala. My passion for salads was inspired by these people, who make lunches non-stop with humility and love in many parts of the crowded cities.

Spicy yogurt raita with tomatoes, cucumber and shallots used to be my favourite salad of all. However, eating fresh cucumber slices with black salt masala and lime juice at the corner of Palika bazaar in New Delhi, or having a spicy salad of bananas, cheekoo, pineapple and guava on the roadside near Chanakya Puri, is a completely different and enjoyable experience.

Bean olathiyathu

This is my own way of preparing beans when I am tired of eating thorans or when someone wants a dish with no coconut. Bean olathiyathu has the flavour of a curry but is dry like a side dish. Any kind of green bean can be used to make this dish, fresh or frozen, but as I'm sure you'll know, fresh is always the best.

serves 4

1 tablespoon oil

1 teaspoon mustard seeds

1 teaspoon urad dal

1 dried red chilli

a few curry leaves

500g/1 lb 2 oz green or string beans, finely chopped

2 tablespoons freshly grated coconut or desiccated coconut

salt

Heat the oil in a large frying pan. Add the mustard seeds, urad dal, chilli and curry leaves. As the mustard seeds begin to pop, add the green or string beans, coconut, a little salt and 2 tablespoons of water. Mix well.

Cover the pan, lower the heat and cook for 10 minutes or until the beans are tender. Serve hot or cold.

Spicy raita

Raita is served as a cooling dish in most Indian states. I've found that having a raita on the menu at Rasa is essential – British people are used to having raitas with Indian meals – and we make them in a number of ways. South Indians like their raitas to have plenty of flavour and colour. This one helps make a meal a spicy treat and has proved most popular with our Indian customers. If you prefer a mild raita, just omit the chillies.

serves 4

200g/7 oz plain yogurt

1 tomato, cubed

50g/2 oz cucumber, cubed

3 fresh green chillies, finely sliced

1.5cm/³/₄ in cube fresh root ginger, finely chopped

a few sprigs of fresh coriander, chopped

a pinch of chilli powder

In a large bowl, combine the yogurt, tomato, cucumber, green chillies and ginger. Mix well, then garnish with the coriander and chilli powder. Serve cold.

Spicy fruit and vegetable salad

Since developing my interest in salads, I have visited Ealing Road market in Wembley many times to look at the beautifully displayed tropical fruits and vegetables. They have a number of different fruits like mango, guava, cheekoo and jackfruit and any of these could be used to make this salad. I love to add some chopped fresh shallots tossed with lemon juice and vinegar to this recipe for extra flavour. Serve it as part of a meal or just on its own, which is how I like to eat it.

serves 4

2 medium potatoes

1 medium sweet potato

3 tomatoes

¹/₂ cucumber

2 apples

2 pears

2 oranges

2 bananas

1 tablespoon chat masala

1¹/₂ teaspoons salt

¹/₂ teaspoon chilli powder

2 tablespoons lemon juice

Place the potatoes and sweet potato in a large saucepan and cover with water. Bring to the boil and cook for 15 minutes or until the potatoes are soft. Drain and set aside to cool. Cut the potatoes into bite-sized chunks.

Meanwhile, cut the tomatoes, cucumber, apples and pears into bite-sized chunks and place in a large bowl. Segment the oranges, then cut each segment in half and add to the bowl. Cut the bananas into slices around 1.5cm/³/₄ in thick and toss them into the salad.

Add the potatoes to the other vegetables and fruits in the bowl, then sprinkle on the chat masala, salt and chilli.

Pour the lemon juice over the other ingredients and toss very well using a spoon. Cover the salad and chill slightly before serving.

Guava coconut salad

Last summer my friend Angela brought me an Indian guava and asked me to make something for her that reminds me of Kerala. When I think of my home state, what else would spring to mind but coconut? Although South Indians eat both guava and coconut raw, it is unusual to combine them. Angela loves coconut too, so I devised this salad and have made it many times since then. Today guava is available year-round from many parts of the world.

2 tablespoons oil

1 teaspoon mustard seeds

1 teaspoon urad dal

a few curry leaves

100g/3½ oz shallots, halved

a large pinch of chilli powder

a large pinch of turmeric powder

3 tablespoons lemon juice

3 tablespoons white wine vinegar

50g/2 oz fresh coconut, sliced

1 unripe guava, sliced

salt

Heat the oil in a large frying pan or wok. Add the mustard seeds and, as they begin to pop, add the urad dal and curry leaves. Cook, stirring, until the urad dal turns golden.

Add the shallots and stir-fry for 5 minutes, until the shallots are shiny and translucent.

Stir in the chilli, turmeric and some salt. Add the lemon juice and vinegar, then the coconut slices and mix well.

Remove the pan from the heat and transfer the shallot mixture to a large bowl. Toss with the guava, then serve.

Kerala cucumber and coconut salad

We are not big salad eaters at home, although we do eat a lot of raw fruits and vegetables. One day in 1985, I was passing through Delhi's Palika Park and was fascinated to see people buying raw cucumbers, slit into four and spiced with salt and lemon juice, to eat as a summery afternoon snack. It inspired me to develop this very unusual salad. I love its fresh, revitalising flavour.

serves 4

1 cucumber, peeled and finely chopped

½ fresh coconut, finely sliced or grated

1 carrot, finely chopped

1 tomato, finely chopped

1 fresh green chilli, finely chopped

a small bunch of fresh coriander, finely chopped

2 tablespoons lemon juice

salt

for the dressing:

2 teaspoons oil

1 teaspoon mustard seeds

1 teaspoon cumin seeds

1 dried red chilli, halved

½ teaspoon asafoetida

a few curry leaves

Place the cucumber, coconut, carrot, tomato, green chilli and coriander in a salad bowl and set aside.

To make the dressing, heat the oil in a large frying pan. Add the mustard seeds and, as they begin to pop, add the cumin, dried red chilli, asafoetida and curry leaves. Stir well.

Remove the pan from the heat and pour its contents over the salad. Add the lemon juice and some salt to taste and mix thoroughly. Leave to cool before serving.

Green mango salad

Eating raw mango with freshly ground chilli powder and coconut oil was a childhood habit for me. We would take small packets of chilli powder and oil in our lunch boxes to school. During the lunch break, naughty kids like me used to enjoy throwing stones at the mango trees of the neighbouring houses. When the mangoes fell, we would climb over the walls and steal them. Then it was time for a fabulous mango feast. With the help of the blade that we used to sharpen our school pencils, we cut our mangoes and spiced them before eating. This is a useful technique for making a salad even today, though I no longer have to steal the mangoes!

serves 4

2 tablespoons oil

1 teaspoon mustard seeds

1 teaspoon urad dal

a few curry leaves

100g/3 1/2 oz shallots, halved

a large pinch of chilli powder

a large pinch of turmeric powder

3 tablespoons lemon juice

3 tablespoons white wine vinegar

2 medium-ripe green mangoes, thickly sliced

salt

Heat the oil in a large frying pan or wok. Add the mustard seeds and, as they begin to pop, add the urad dal and curry leaves. Cook, stirring, until the urad dal turns golden.

Add the shallots and stir-fry for 5 minutes, until the shallots are shiny and translucent.

Stir in the chilli, turmeric and some salt, then add the lemon juice, vinegar and mangoes. Mix well and cook until the mangoes are just tender.

Remove the pan from the heat and transfer the mixture to a large serving bowl. Serve cold.

desserts and drinks

desserts

Sweets are one of the most glorious aspects of Indian cooking. A happy celebration is not complete without a traditional sweet and each region has its own unique, memorable desserts. Today, Indian desserts are widely known and available all over the world, thanks to the celebrations and restaurants of expatriates. These sweets and desserts can be offered at any time of day, after meals, as a morning or afternoon snack, or simply as a surprise gesture of joy and sweetness.

Just like the other foods we cook, sweets vary not only from state to state but from community to community and function to function. However, across all four states, South Indian homes are unanimous in their choice of payasams for special occasions. They are considered indispensable and made everywhere using a variety of styles and ingredients, including rice, lentils, banana, jackfruit and mung beans. Most often we use jaggery as the sweetener, plus coconut milk and spices to distinguish the dish from other Indian desserts.

In Kerala, people fondly remember a good taste for a long time and payasam is eagerly anticipated at wedding feasts. My memory of a favourite milk payasam called palada pradhaman was a delightful experience watching an old Brahmin cook on my sister's wedding day. The event was not just for 100 or 200 people – we had almost 1500 guests and it was the largest marriage in our family. What I remember most about the party was the taste of that white milky pudding with thin, chewy rice chips, sweet and delicious. Even today, when I go back home, I look forward to finding that chef and asking him the favour of making the same pudding yet again, and being able to watch him do it. That's why we Keralans believe it is very important to know who cooks the puddings, and you can often hear people discussing and comparing the sweets they have had over many years cooked by many different people.

We have desserts inherited from other communities in India too, including the halwa from Calicut, a Muslim-populated town in north Kerala. The preparation of halwa is time-consuming and labour-intensive, so we prefer to buy it from teashops or bakeries, but there are easier desserts to make in the home such as soft carrot halwa and semolina kesari. We also enjoy pancakes, crisp sweet munchies, soft melting candies, syrups and honey, all in a variety of colours, textures and flavours – that's why we are the sweetest people in India.

Jackfruit payasam

I recommend this spectacular payasam for small functions or celebrations. Jackfruit is a huge fruit with an unusual taste and grows widely in Kerala. When unripe, it is used as a vegetable in curries and dry dishes; when ripe it is made into a wide range of desserts. Keralan cooks like experimenting with it. My mum makes jam and fudge from jackfruit as well as this delicious payasam. Once the flesh is removed from the seeds, jackfruit is easy to cook with but easiest of all is to buy the fresh prepacked slices sold in Asian grocers.

serves 4

8 tablespoons ghee
25g/1 oz raw cashew nuts
25g/1 oz raisins
250g/9 oz jackfruit, finely sliced
150g/5 oz jaggery
250g/9 oz coconut milk
1/2 teaspoon ground cardamom

Heat 3 tablespoons of the ghee in a frying pan and sauté the cashew nuts and raisins until the nuts turn brown and the raisins puff up. Drain on kitchen paper and set aside.

In a medium saucepan, simmer the jackfruit in 450ml/16 fl oz of water for 5 minutes or until the fruit is well cooked. Add the jaggery and cook over a moderate heat, stirring continuously, for another 5 minutes.

Add the remaining ghee to the jackfruit mixture and cook over a medium heat, stirring continuously until the ghee is thoroughly blended.

Lower the heat under the pan and stir the coconut milk into the mixture. Simmer for another few minutes, then add the cardamom and the sautéed cashews and raisins. Stir well and serve hot.

Ari payasam

Wherever you travel in Kerala, you can't miss the passion for festivals, celebrations and food. On such occasions, payasam – a pudding made from rice, milk, jaggery, coconut milk and nuts – is indispensable and cooked in many forms. Ari or rice payasam is my mum's speciality whenever we have an auspicious gathering at home with close family members. Although she used to make many payasams, I liked this one best because my first assignment in the kitchen (on Dad's orders) was to help her in making it. I really enjoyed that first lesson. Ari payasam is also one of the easiest payasams to make.

serves 4

75g/3 oz ghee
25g/1 oz raw cashew nuts
25g/1 oz raisins
1.2 litres/2 pints milk
100g/3½ oz basmati rice
100g/3½ oz jaggery
100g/3½ oz coconut milk

Heat 25g/1 oz of the ghee in a frying pan and sauté the cashews and raisins together until the cashews are golden and the raisins puff up. Drain on kitchen paper and set aside.

Heat the milk in a medium saucepan. Add the rice and simmer gently for 15 minutes until the rice is well cooked. Add the jaggery and cook for a further 5 minutes. Add the remaining ghee and stir until it has been thoroughly combined with the rice mixture.

Lower the heat under the saucepan right down and stir in the coconut milk, then the sautéed cashews and raisins. Remove the pan from the heat and serve immediately, or leave to cool and serve the pudding cold.

Kerala mango ice cream

Kerala produces an amazing selection of mangoes – at my childhood home we grew at least five different varieties – and (just like the state's bananas) they vary in taste depending on the area in which they are grown. Keralan mangoes vary enormously in shape and skin colour compared to their northern counterparts, which tend to be bright golden yellow. Our mangoes usually have green skin that remains so until the fruit is too ripe. I first had this mango ice cream at Ms Mini Jacob's house when I was studying in Trivandrum. It was so amazing and I asked her straight away how to make it, but it has taken me some years to get it exactly right for the restaurants.

makes about 1 litre/1¾ pints

1 tablespoon custard powder
3 tablespoons caster sugar
450ml/16 fl oz milk
425g/15 oz fresh or canned mango purée
100ml/3½ fl oz double cream, lightly whipped
sliced mango, to decorate (optional)

Mix together the custard powder and sugar in a saucepan. Pour in a little of the milk and stir to dissolve the custard powder and sugar completely, then add the remaining milk, stirring until no lumps remain.

Place the saucepan over medium heat and bring the custard to the boil, stirring continuously. When the mixture has thickened enough to coat the back of a spoon, remove the pan from the heat and immediately place it in a bowl of ice-cold water. Stir continuously until the custard cools down.

When the mixture is cold, fold the mango purée and whipped double cream into the custard. Pour the mixture into a large plastic container, cover and place in the freezer.

After 20 minutes, take the container out of the freezer and give the mixture a thorough whisk before returning to the freezer to freeze for another 20 minutes. Repeat this at least 3 or 4 times to prevent ice crystals forming in the mixture.

Remove the ice cream from the freezer 15 minutes before serving (or less, depending on the heat of the kitchen) to soften it slightly. Decorate with sliced mango, if using.

Banana sago pudding

Mrs Nair used to make this dessert for Onam celebrations. I used to run to her place to eat this pudding during the holidays, as the taste was so unusual compared to what we had at home. It's very easy to make and a great way to use up ripe bananas, which we tend to have a lot of in Kerala. Mrs Nair particularly recommended using the sugar variety of banana and fresh coconut for this recipe. In Kerala, I would eat it as an afternoon teatime snack as well as a dessert.

serves 4

3 tablespoons sago

12 large pieces banana leaves

4 ripe bananas

50g/2 oz jaggery, cubed

25g/1 oz white sugar

1 teaspoon vanilla essence

4 tablespoons freshly grated or desiccated coconut

Wash and soak the sago in water according to the packet instructions – typically for 1 hour. Meanwhile, dip the banana leaves in hot water to soften them, then set aside until ready to cook. Also, prepare a steamer with water ready to bring to the boil.

In a mixing bowl, mash the bananas. Add the jaggery, white sugar and vanilla essence and mix thoroughly. Drain the sago and stir it into the banana mixture.

Bring the water in the steamer to a boil. Place a spoonful of the mixture on each piece of banana leaf, then sprinkle 1 teaspoon of coconut in the middle. Fold the banana leaves up into parcels, place in the steamer and cook for 15 minutes. Undo the parcels and serve hot.

Nendra rasa

Ripe plantain has very black skin and the sweetest flesh. It is the best fruit to use for stuffed desserts such as this one because it holds together after steaming. This recipe comes from my friend Pushpa, an excellent home cook, who came to help me during our first Rasa festival. It was the first time I had cooked for a huge function and it gave me a great opportunity to learn from her. She claims that this is a special dish from Kannoor in North Kerala, but I never had it when I was living in Kerala. It was a pleasant surprise to learn something new and we have made it at Rasa ever since.

serves 4

500g/1 lb 2 oz ripe plantain, unpeeled

100g/3½ oz semolina

5 tablespoons vegetable oil

for the stuffing:

1 tablespoon ghee

100g/3½ oz broken cashew nuts

100g/3½ oz raisins

100g/3½ oz freshly grated or desiccated coconut

2 tablespoons sugar

Wash the unpeeled plantain, then trim off the top and bottom of the fruit and cut each one in half. Place in a steamer (or a colander over a saucepan of boiling water) and steam for 1 hour or until the plantain is soft and the skin cracks.

Meanwhile, make the stuffing. Heat the ghee in a frying pan over a medium heat. Add the cashews, sauté until golden, then drain on kitchen paper. Add a little more ghee to the pan if required and return to the heat. Add the raisins, cook until they swell, then drain and set aside to cool. In a bowl, combine the cashews, raisins, coconut and sugar and mix well.

When the plantains are cooked, remove them from the steamer and leave to cool for 5 minutes. Peel and mash the plantain flesh very finely. When cool enough to handle, divide the plantain mash into portions: either 8 small portions giving 2 pieces per person, or 4 large portions giving 1 piece each.

Roll into balls, then make a hole in the middle and fill with the stuffing. Smooth the plantain over to seal the hole, then roll the balls in semolina to coat thoroughly. Set aside for 5 minutes to harden.

Heat the oil in a frying pan and fry the plantain balls until the semolina is crisp and golden. Serve hot or cold with fresh cream or ice cream.

Pistachio kulfi

Kulfi – a type of ice cream – is a well-known dessert in restaurants around the world. The best kulfi I have ever had was on the streets of New Delhi. On that city's hot summer days, you never get tired of cold sweets or drinks. North Indian people love milky sweets and make them richly flavoured with nuts and spices. In the South, kulfi is a relatively new import and Keralan people are just beginning to relish the best Indian ice creams. This method of making kulfi is one I learned from a close friend while working in a Delhi hotel, but people use different methods according to their communities and experience. My favourite nuts are pistachios and I particularly like kulfi made from them.

makes about 2.5 litres/4¹/₂ pints

4 litres/7 pints milk
1 tablespoon rice flour
175g/6 oz sugar
50g/2 oz ground pistachio nuts
150ml/5 fl oz double cream, lightly whipped
a few drops of rose water
25g/1 oz unsalted pistachio nuts, crushed

Pour the milk into a large, heavy-based saucepan, bring it to the boil, then lower the heat slightly and simmer briskly, uncovered, for about 45 minutes until it has thickened and reduced to half its original quantity.

Remove the milk from the heat and allow it to cool slightly. Dissolve the rice flour in a little of the thickened milk and pour it back into the pan. Cook, stirring continuously, over a low heat for 15 minutes until the mixture is the consistency of a pouring batter.

Add the sugar and stir until completely dissolved. Remove the pan from the heat, cover and leave to cool completely.

When cool, stir the ground pistachios into the mixture, then fold in the cream, rose water and crushed pistachios. Pour the mixture into a large plastic container and place in the freezer for 1 hour.

Remove the kulfi from the freezer and whisk it thoroughly. Return to the freezer for another hour. Repeat this process another two times, then leave the kulfi in the freezer for several hours or overnight.

Allow the kulfi to soften for about 5 minutes at room temperature before serving.

Neyyappam

The Sabari Mala temple comes to mind when I think of neyyappam because it offers this sweet to pilgrims. Although I have only been to this unusual temple twice, I've eaten the sweet many times because my father would visit every year and bring home bags of neyyappam for family and friends. Occasionally Mum would make it as a snack for afternoon tea when we came home from school. Whenever I want to relive my childhood, this reminds me of those special days. At the restaurants, we serve it with a creamy sauce made with cashew nuts.

serves 4

150g/5 oz jaggery
275g/10 oz rice flour
60g/2½ oz plain flour
2 tablespoons freshly grated or desiccated coconut
1 tablespoon butter
1 banana, mashed
½ teaspoon ground cardamom
ghee, for deep-frying

In a large saucepan, heat the jaggery over a medium heat till it melts, then set aside to cool.

Meanwhile, in a large bowl, combine the rice flour, plain flour, coconut and butter. Mix well, adding just enough water to form a smooth batter. Stir in the mashed banana and cardamom, then set aside for 1 hour.

Heat a generous quantity of ghee in a neyyappam griddle, deep frying pan or wok. If using the neyyappam griddle, pour a spoonful of the batter into each hollow and cook until browned underneath. If using a frying pan or wok, divide the batter into golf-ball sized pieces, then flatten into a disk shape and drop in the ghee. Using a long fork, turn to cook on the other side. Remove and set aside to drain while you repeat with the remaining batter. Serve hot or cold.

Badam halwa

Rasa's sweet specialist Siva Prasad introduced this distinctive almond fudge to me. Badam halwa is a rich sweet well liked in India and goes well with ice cream. This is the correct method of making it, though rather time consuming. Ready-made almond powder will save you some time, but using whole almonds results in fudge that tastes far better. At no stage should the mixture be allowed to stick to the bottom of the pan and scorch as it will ruin the taste of the halwa.

serves 4

225g/8 oz unblanched almonds
570ml/1 pint milk
225g/8 oz sugar
225g/8 oz ghee
100g/3½ oz crushed almonds, to decorate

Place the unblanched almonds in a large bowl and cover with around 1.5 litres/2½ pints of water. Leave to soak overnight. Next day, the almonds should have doubled in size. Drain and skin the almonds and place in a blender or food processor. Working at low speed, grind the nuts to a smooth paste, gradually adding the milk.

In a large saucepan, dissolve the sugar in 150ml/5 fl oz of water. Bring to the boil and boil rapidly for about 10 minutes or until the volume of liquid has reduced by half. Add the ground almond mixture, lower the heat and simmer for 1 hour until thick, stirring very frequently to prevent scorching.

In a separate saucepan, melt the ghee. Slowly pour a little ghee into the almond mixture and stir continuously until it has been completely absorbed into the paste.

Within a few minutes, the paste will start to release ghee. As soon as that happens, pour in a little more of the melted ghee and once again stir continuously until the ghee has been absorbed. Repeat this process until all the ghee has been incorporated and the rich almond paste is glossy.

Transfer the paste to a shallow cake tin and spread it out to a thickness of no more than 1.5cm/¾ in. Leave to cool and, as soon as it begins to set, cut the halwa into squares and sprinkle with the crushed almonds. Serve warm or cold.

Carrot halwa

When I lived in Delhi, carrot halwa was considered a treat in winter, when we'd order it in little teashops or sweet places. Most of the time, however, I found it dry or too heavy, as it contained lots of ghee. This recipe is a South Indian rendition of carrot halwa, made with a little ghee but also with milk to give a moist texture. I love eating it with coconut ice cream.

serves 8

100g/3½ oz ghee

25g/1 oz raisins

25g/1 oz cashew nuts

250g/9 oz grated carrot

200ml/7 fl oz milk

150g/5 oz sugar

a pinch of powdered cardamom

In a frying pan, heat 2 tablespoons of the ghee and fry the raisins and cashews until the nuts are golden. Set aside.

Heat 50g/2 oz of the ghee in a kadai, wok or deep saucepan. Add the carrot and fry for 5 minutes, stirring. Pour in the milk and simmer over a moderate heat for 10 minutes.

Stir the sugar and remaining ghee into the carrot mixture. Continue cooking for another 5 minutes until the mixture is soft and well blended. Add the raisins, cashews and cardamom. Serve hot or cold.

drinks

As elsewhere in the world, hospitality in Kerala is expressed by offering a drink to guests. This custom is a must in all Indian homes. The drink can be as simple as a glass of cool, clear water, but beyond this humble offering is a wonderful variety of non-alcoholic drinks.

Throughout India the most popular drink is fresh lime juice. Street vendors make it from syrups made of sugar or salt and herbs and it is available on nearly every corner and railway station. Although it is traditionally made using plain water, soda and carbonated mineral water are also very refreshing mixers. The small boys and girls carrying their little trays of ready-made lime juice drinks are an unforgettable sight when travelling in buses or trains in Kerala and, since the weather is hot most of the year, they do good business.

I have always been fascinated by the range of fruit juices available in India. On a hot summer day in Kerala we tend to drink lots of tender coconut water; fruit juices tend only to be made from red grapes and mango, and mostly we serve them plain. In the North, however, they have a fantastic selection of natural juices including apple, carrot, cheekoo and banana varieties and they often add fresh spicy flavourings such as mint, ginger and cardamom to turn them into more exotic drinks.

Milk and yogurt shakes are a real treat too. In Kerala we like our yogurt drinks to be salty but in the North they have it sweet most of the time. During the mango season, mango shakes and lassi are unavoidable. Apple banana lassi is the one that does most justice to the incredible variety of bananas available in Kerala.

If you asked me to choose just one out of all the interesting drinks available, I would say the favourite drink for a Keralan man would be a nice hot tea, any time of day. We are the tea drinkers of India when it comes to numbers of cups per day. When most people come to visit, they won't leave until they've been offered a nice cup of homemade tea with a strong milky flavour, but I do have one friend, called Manju, who always asks for, 'Black coffee, please!'

Carrot ginger mint juice

Healthy fresh fruit juices are a speciality of North India and I had plenty of them during my time in Delhi. Carrot juice particularly fascinated me because in Kerala we do not use carrots in cooking as much as our North Indian counterparts. Also, the inclusion of spices such as ginger and mint in the drink was something new to me at the time and I thought it heavenly. It was always a treat to go to the juice bars on wages day and spend all my money on these drinks, then starve for the next week.

serves 4

15 carrots

5cm/2 in piece fresh root ginger

2 tablespoons mint leaves

2 tablespoons sugar (optional)

crushed ice, to serve

Put the carrots, ginger and mint together through a juice extractor. Transfer the mixture to a jug and add sugar to taste if desired, whisking until the sugar is dissolved.

Serve cold over crushed ice.

Jeera vellam

At lunchtime, in any Keralan home you visit, they will offer you a glass of jeera water. This practice is based on the Ayurvedic tradition of drinking to aid digestion and control thirst. My mum makes jeera water everyday; we used to drink it after every meal and Dad would take it with him to his shop daily. It is recommended to lower the heat in the body and we were taught to drink it hot even on a hot day. In fact, there is a Sanskrit saying: 'drink hot when it's hot'. Crush the cumin seeds slightly in your palm before adding them to the boiling water as this will bring out their flavour.

1 tablespoon cumin seeds

In a saucepan, bring 1 litre/1¾ pints of water to the boil. Add the cumin seeds and simmer for 5 minutes.

Remove from the heat and serve hot or cold.

Mango lassi

The most popular drink at Rasa restaurants is mango lassi. In India, while lassi is served throughout the country, each area has a different recipe. For example, Southerners enjoy spicy, aromatic buttermilk lassis, but the people of Bombay and Delhi drink sweet and mango-flavoured lassis. Today lassi is so popular that you can buy it ready-made in supermarkets, but for the best flavour I recommend making it yourself with fresh home-made yogurt and a nice Alphonso mango, which is widely available in stores. If you make the lassi too thick, it can be heavy as a drink but will still be good for dessert! I always make it light and thin and add a lot of milk.

serves 4

250g/9 oz plain yogurt
200g/7 oz mango, peeled and cut into chunks
100g/3 1/2 oz mango pulp
125ml/4 fl oz milk
4 teaspoons white sugar
1/4 teaspoon crushed cardamom
crushed ice, to serve

Place the yogurt, mango, mango pulp, milk, sugar and cardamom in a blender. Process for 2 minutes or until thick and smooth.

Pour the lassi over the crushed ice and serve immediately. Without the crushed ice, the lassi can be stored in the fridge for up to 24 hours.

mangoes

Passion fruit cordial

The favourite way of eating passion fruit in Kerala is to just cut open the shell and eat the flesh with a tiny bit of sugar. I didn't taste my first passion fruit cordial until I visited Guruvayoor Krishna temple, which used to have a small shop serving juices and fresh fruits to the pilgrims for the temple offering. In those days it was one of the few places that sold passion fruit drinks, but today many people make them at home to offer to guests instead of tea. In this recipe it is best to use fresh passion fruit rather than frozen pulp, but it will take a while to extract the juice.

makes about 1.35 litres/2¼ pints
570ml/1 pint fresh passion fruit pulp
1 teaspoon fresh ginger juice
a small pinch of salt
2 tablespoons sugar, or to taste
crushed ice, to serve

Pour the passion fruit pulp into a blender with 700ml/1¼ pints of water. Add the ginger juice and salt, then taste and add sugar as required. Blend until the sugar has dissolved. Serve cold over crushed ice. The remaining cordial can be kept in the refrigerator for up to 1 week.

passion fruit cordial (left) and mango lassi (page 151)

Menu planner

menu 1 starters
Koonu bhajia *(page 31)*
Plain dosa *(page 24)*
Coconut and tamarind chutney
  (page 38)

main course
Rasa biryani *(page 60)*
Bhindi thoran *(page 118)*
Kayi korma curry *(page 70)*
Kerala paratha *(page 49)*

dessert
Kerala mango ice cream *(page 138)*

menu 2 starters
Mixed vegetable pakoda *(page 31)*
Mushroom and cashew nut samosas
  (page 27)
Rava cake *(page 34)*
Tomato chutney *(page 41)*

main course
Cheera thayir curry *(page 82)*
Kadala curry *(page 89)*
Onion chapatti *(page 51)*
Curd rice *(page 65)*

dessert
Badam halwa *(page 145)*

from left to right: mushroom and cashew nut samosas (page 27), bhindi thoran (page 118) and Kerala mango ice cream (page 138)

menu 3 starters
Pappadavadai *(page 17)*
Pal katti porichattu *(page 30)*
Chilli and ginger pickle *(page 45)*

main course
Cauliflower and potato curry
  (page 84)
Vendekka cheera kozhambu
  (page 83)
Papaya thoran *(page 121)*
Peas pilau rice *(page 63)*
Kerala paratha *(page 49)*

dessert
Carrot halwa *(page 146)*

menu 4 starters
Parippu soup *(page 100)*
Rasa idli *(page 32)*
Coconut and tamarind chutney
  (page 38)

main course
Avial *(page 69)*
Ulli theeyal *(page 76)*
Cabbage curry *(page 80)*
Potato podimas *(page 110)*
Black pepper rice *(page 58)*
Sannas *(page 54)*

dessert
Jackfruit payasam *(page 136)*

menu 5 starters
Potato and coriander vadai *(page 28)*
Pal katti porichattu *(page 30)*
Murukku *(page 21)*
Tomato chutney *(page 41)*

main course
Yam in yogurt sauce *(page 87)*
Veluthulli curry *(page 77)*
Broccoli and coconut curry *(page 71)*
Drumstick thoran *(page 116)*
Guava coconut salad *(page 127)*
Bisi bele rice *(page 59)*

dessert
Pistachio kulfi *(page 143)*

feast menu starters
Medhu vadai *(page 29)*
Koonu bhajia *(page 31)*
Mixed vegetable pakoda *(page 31)*
Tomato chutney *(page 41)*

main course
Kochi dosa *(page 25)*
Avial *(page 69)*
Cucumber curry *(page 72)*
Ulli theeyal *(page 76)*
Peas pilau rice *(page 63)*
Vegetable paratha *(page 50)*

dessert
Banana sago pudding *(page 140)*
Jackfruit payasam *(page 136)*

rasa restaurants

Rasa's first restaurant, a small premises in Stoke Newington, north London, was opened by Das Sreedharan in 1994 to immediate acclaim from locals and restaurant critics. The pure vegetarian menu comprising authentic home-style Keralan dishes was unlike any other in London and a magnet for Britain's curry-loving public. So high was the standard of cooking that leading chefs specialising in other cuisines would travel right across the city to enjoy dinner at Rasa, a name based on the Sanskrit word for 'taste'.

With queues of eager customers forming outside the door each evening, the restaurant was a hit and Das found the confidence and backing to open in the heart of London's West End. Rasa W1 is a larger premises, with more sophisticated décor. Its location in Dering Street, just off London's famous Oxford Street, proved to be a prime position to bring Rasa's vegetarian food to an even wider, and appreciative, public.

In 1999 Das decided to part from the pure vegetarian format of his first two restaurants. Even though he personally remains a committed vegetarian, he is also on a mission to bring all the traditional cooking of Kerala to a broader audience, and this includes the dishes of Indian communities that enjoy eating fish and meat. Rasa Samudra in Charlotte Street, a short walk from the Dering Street premises, was the first Indian restaurant in the UK to specialise in seafood. The name means 'taste of the ocean' and the venue surprised many critics, who were so unfamiliar with the authentic seafood cooking of Kerala that they found themselves drawing inappropriate comparisons with the contrastingly mild vegetarian dishes they had come to know and love at the original Rasa.

The year 2001 saw Das exploring yet more new ideas, but also in a sense coming full circle. Back in Stoke Newington, where he continues to live, he opened Rasa Travancore across the road from the original Rasa. It is another highly successful innovation on the London dining scene: the first restaurant based on the cooking of Kerala's Christian community and one with a menu including meat dishes. Critical acclaim was instantaneous, but Das has never been one to rest on his laurels and he continues to plan further openings to bring real Keralan food to an ever wider, perhaps worldwide, audience.

Index

Note: page numbers in *italics* refer to illustrations

Acknowledgements

Thanks to: my friend Jenni Muir for all her help in putting together this book, even at the last minute; my manager and close friend Preeta for her contribution and support during those busiest months of my life; chefs Narayanan, Prasad and Madhu for their valuable tips and time when I most needed them; Vinod Kumar, my banker friend, for his all-round talent and helping me out with his expertise; Elaine Collins for her kind understanding of my non-stop work; Angela who has made it look easy to smile and work; all those great individuals whom I mention in the book – their devotion to cooking inspired me and I try hard to follow them; Vanessa Courtier, Sunil Vijayakar and Pete Cassidy for their excellent work to make this a great Indian cookbook; and last, but not least, Heather Holden-Brown for having faith in me and my cooking.